# In Other Words

## A Collection of Thoughts & Columns

By Karen Dumas

**Outskirts Press, Inc.**
**Denver, Colorado**

Outskirts Press, Inc.
http://www.outskirtspress.com

ISBN: 978-1-4327-1130-6

Outskirts Press and the "OP" logo are trademarks belonging to Outskirts Press, Inc.

PRINTED IN THE UNITED STATES OF AMERICA

*This book is dedicated to my late mother, Fannye*

iii

# Table of Contents

# Chapter 10: **& Then Some**

- Respect Is Timeless
- The High Price of Freedom
- Black? Proud?
- Just One Last Time
- Right To Live…Not Just Life
- Mistaken Demise: Care, Concern
- Hands Off My SUV
- Outside?!?!?
- Once Upon A Time, There Was A Tomorrow
- Learning to Share In A Selfish World

# *Acknowledgements*

Writing has been a life long activity for me, from school-work to professional assignments and all in between. Being able to publish those writings in a book format has long been a dream and a plan, which is now a reality.

The beginning is always the appropriate place to start, and in doing so I have to acknowledge my late mother, Fannye Dumas, for always making me write correctly and encouraging me to fine tune my interest; Mr. Joseph Cadarieu, my former religion teacher at East Catholic High School in Detroit, Michigan, who recognized my love of and talent for writing, and gave me a blank book (that I still have) and encouraged me to write my own story in life—literally and figuratively!

There have been more people along the way that could fill these pages, each of whom have contributed to this process and my success, whether they knew they were doing so or not.

Certainly, thanks are due to my family—husband Timothy Cook and children Kirby & Jason, who all are a constant support system and reminder to press on, no pun intended. Much appreciation to Karen Love and Sam Logan of The Michigan Chronicle and The Michigan Front Page newspapers who gave me a forum and outlet for my thoughts and opinions in a regular column, and then permission to share some of those columns in this book.

And the three published authors who pushed me over the edge: Darrious Hilmon, who said the magic words that moved me from plan to progress, Sylvia Hubbard of Motown Writers for her support in completing this project, and

Elizabeth Atkins who *always* took the time to share insights and tips that continued to move me toward completion.

Thanks to Elena Farmer for her keen graphic art skills, Stacie Clayton and my sister Carmen Robinson for more than I can list, Dr. Robert Thomas for getting it all together, and Monica Morgan for photography that never fails.

There have been more people along the way that could fill these pages, each of whom have contributed to this process and my success, whether they knew they were doing so or not. From family and friends, to strangers and enemies, everyone has moved me—gently or forcibly—one step closer to my goal.

I attempted to name those who were immediately influential, but will defer to a practice of the late Coleman A. Young, former Mayor of the City of Detroit. I will not try to name all of those whom I want to acknowledge or thank, as in doing so will inevitably but unintentionally forget someone. That, as Mayor Young would say, would make those mentioned happy, but disappoint those forgotten.

So, you know who you are—yeah, you, too—and I sincerely appreciate you all. Really.

And, to *you* who have taken the leap of faith by buying and now reading this book, I sincerely thank you as well and hope that you enjoy reading it as much I enjoyed writing it!

In this collection of comments & columns, I first take a look at the social side of our lives. The things that help to shape who we are and what we do from the societal side— education, entertainment, politics and social practices.

We all recognize these and other factors in our lives, but rarely assess their impact, and motivation for our being…or not. It has always been my practice both in writing and on the air to look at things from perspectives different than the ones usually tossed around in the media and conversations. Asking, "what if" and "why not" sparks discussion and breeds solutions like you wouldn't believe. Casually, taking on the topical aspect of issues and incidents is entertaining, but it is far more rewarding when you tackle them with intelligent discussion and an open mind. You'd be amazed at what we can think, speak and accomplish when we are receptive to another –and sometimes differing--opinion. I then take a look at the more personal side of our lives. Those things that help to shape who we are and what we do from a personal and emotional perspective—family, friends, and even strangers. The places we go, the people we meet or watch, and the things that we do, or wish that we could.

Everyone and everything leaves an imprint, if you allow them. That can be good, or bad, depending on the circumstances and influencing factors.

What we watch, wear, hear, see and say all matter. How much so, is up to you.

# Chapter One:
## *Speak Up*

*Speaking up makes a difference.*

*Saying nothing can validate injustices or even innocent mistakes.*

*Of all the weapons and gifts that are exchanged between us, nothing is more powerful than words. They bite, embrace, pull us closer or push us farther apart; when used correctly, they convey grace, intelligence and appeal.*

*When used incorrectly, they reveal ignorance, tactlessness and disdain.*

*Yet, when used in fairness and love, words are the most constructive of vehicles. They inform, inspire, educate and encourage.*

# SILENCE IS NOT A SOLUTION

While hosting *The Art Blackwell Show* recently, I mentioned an incident that occurred at a local school. Without ever mentioning the name of the school, I talked about how this incident took up quite a bit of time at a recent parent meeting, and how the very nature of incidents that are occurring with our young people dictate that we as parents and a community must aggressively communicate with them about such things. Well, it was later brought to my attention that some felt as though I should not have even brought the incident up on the air, especially since my daughter attends the school and perhaps there were some more positive things that I could have been talking about. I disagree, because nothing is more important than prevention, and building understanding and trust through communication with our children.

Issues like pregnancy; oral sex, homosexuality, drug use, bullying, and outright violence are the issues at hand for our young people today. They are doing it, seeing others doing it, hearing about it, or being victimized by it. It is taking place in schools and other places that some would feel more comfortable telling themselves that it's not. But, the reality is that it is happening, and in public schools, private schools, the city and suburbs to boot. And, pretending that it is not occurring, and then not talking about it, won't help to solve the problem.

Societies, and especially the African-American community, have long shunned discussions about domestic violence, suicide, and sexual abuse for reasons that stem far back into the cultural viscera. Pretending that these and other issues didn't exist has placed an emotional load on thousands of individuals, and a community that can no longer afford the burden of silence.

We talk too often about helping our children to grow into responsible adults. We want them to be well educated, successful and hopefully better than we are. But, that is not possible by pretending that our children's only dilemmas are limited to lunch selections and music choices. Growing up presented each of us with predicaments that we thought we could successfully navigate on our own. Yet, our challenges of yesterday pale in comparison with those faced by today's youth.

A technologically advanced society that makes information, access, and mass communication available at our fingertips makes conversations around a dinner table impossible, if not obsolete. So, ignoring the elephants in the room only make bad matters worse, and resolutions impossible. We can help our young people get through some of these trying times, and in turn help ourselves. But we need to be as accessible as the lures and temptations that greet them on a regular basis. And, at the very least we must acknowledge that of all the options we have and solutions that we can find and use, silence is not one of them.

## SOME LEAVE ME SPEECHLESS

Everybody is in an uproar about the alleged comments made by a high school principal about some of his students—that they would never amount to anything, and more remarks of the same. Well, certainly in a leadership role, these comments, if made, were inappropriate. But the reality is, the observations are, generally, not necessarily untrue nor, his feelings alone. Many think the same, but just don't say anything.

I have been wondering all week about how to talk about the increasingly disappointing behavior that's all too apparent, but really didn't know what to say. Not just poor behavior amongst young people, but the grown ones, too. Folks appear passive, nonchalant, uncaring, disrespectful and overall fine with their apparent compromised role in life. I'm talking about those black folks who make it embarrassing to share with them a culture or any history. You know who they are. They are loud in their posture and presentation— in mouth and appearance. And, to make bad matters worse, speak incorrectly in that loudness. They are cussing out their children or strangers, complaining about something or anything, and just plain pathetic. It has nothing to do with economics, because being broke shouldn't make you rude nor be an excuse for ignorance. I don't know what or who to blame, but it has got to stop. It's not everybody, but it has become more of the norm than the exception, and that is the problem.

Reports, like the one in the *New York Times* last week about the declining social and economic positions of African-American males in America, continue to flood our media outlets. A recent *Newsweek* article highlighted the plight of an African-American female doctor who others— even those who look like her—refused to acknowledge or believe is a **real** doctor. Yet, skipping school, buying rims and plans to buy "Easter clothes" (*whatever those are*) continue to remain priorities over education and social and economic awareness and responsibility. The focus is on false pride rather than progress, and excuses rather than excellence. What in the hell is wrong with you people? Yes, you people—those who refuse to acknowledge that their circumstances are the results of no or poor decisions, and not bad luck or of someone else not doing something for them.

4

Maybe it's time that someone spoke up, and said those things that many others think and refuse to say in public. Maybe it needs to be known that how things are going are not where they should be headed. Perhaps it is time that we all stop pretending that the band-aid approach to our social gunshot wound is working, because clearly it is not.

I hate to admit it, but many of these things have me shaking my head and wondering what to do, and asking if and how things will ever really change. The solutions seem simple— a reprioritization of values; focusing on the future and working towards getting there; putting education and family first; and placing financial needs above wants. But, apparently that is easier said than done. Sure, the system is broken, too, but that should not be an excuse to which an entire race of people succumbs.

So, perhaps this principal was fed up with what he saw and truly felt. I know that I am, and can only hope that many others are, too. As America continues to crumble socially and economically, it is time for those who don't get it, to truly try to begin figuring it out. And, if they still don't, let it not be because the ones who do get it didn't say so.


## HEAR HOW LOUD WE WHISPER

There are two potential major fallouts of the Don Imus incident involving the Rutgers female basketball players, one being the demise of the rap industry as we know it today, and the other a stark reminder of just how silent the black voice actually is in this country.

The Hip-Hop industry has emerged as one of the most profitable musical genres for African-Americans. In spite of the limited to non-existent control and ownership of distribution and broadcast entities, African-Americans have gained and maintained a profitable presence as a result of Hip-Hop, an industry fueled by self-degrading images and lyrics.

Ironically, the cover story of last week's Jet Magazine had Hip-Hop icon, Nas, asking the question, albeit metaphorically, or perhaps prophetically, if Hip-Hop was dead. After the uprising of African-Americans in response to Imus' comments, it may very well be or well on its way.

White America, without question or compromise, controls distribution and broadcast outlets. With criticisms resulting in the firing of Imus from terrestrial radio, the conversation has now turned to the use of the same racist, sexist, and misogynist lyrics that make up the bulk of Hip-Hop today. If we can't do it, they say, should we allow you to do so?

Critics are shouting that they have been complaining about these offensive and degrading lyrics, yet no one has listened or provided them a stage to do so. Left to church pulpits, community stoops and a couple of low wattage AM stations, the message has fallen on a few ears, at best. But, now, they have America's attention because it has infiltrated their comfort zone, removing what more than 3million listeners and viewers regularly embraced as acceptable.

But, this attention may have a boomerang effect: Imus will inevitably turn up on Satellite Radio without much interruption in his format or income; Rappers will now become the high profile target of those who disagreed with Imus' comments; and Black America will be reminded of its limited voice through lack of ownership and commitment to what is right and fair by those who are in a decision making, but check collecting, position.

The few African-American owned broadcast stations and newspapers should now be reminded that they have a responsibility to the community they serve beyond making money at the expense of that same community. Decision makers in key positions at broadcast entities must now assume the role of Al—Roker, not Sharpton—in speaking up and out without fear about those things that are wrong. And, that community must now stand behind those willing to raise their voices and level of expectations in terms of entertainment and information. If not, our voices will remain a whisper and the real music may otherwise go unheard.

## WORDS HAVE RIGHT, LIFE AND MEANING OF THEIR OWN

I have written before about words and freedom, and now I can combine them both. It seems that the argument of when and if words can and should be used has taken on a global conversation of its own. The New York City Council unanimously passed a resolution banning use of the "N" word. Councilman Leroy Comrie, who sponsored the resolution, said that the symbolic measure was to spark discussion on the blatant and disrespectful use and impact of the word. Doesn't everybody.

However, on The BBC's *World Have Your Say*, an international call-in radio show on NPR, people from all over the world, while supporting the discontinued use of the word, warned against the attempt to impose a restriction in a country centered on freedom. The question lingered, "*Where and how would it end?*" The First Amendment gives permission otherwise.

In South Africa, the "K" word, which is equivalent to the "N" word here, is indeed illegal, as it constitutes "hate language." But, then what doesn't or can't constitute such, depending upon the intent and interpretation of the user?

Some of the callers went on to suggest that the "B" word and "H" word, those derogatory words of female orientation, also be banned. What about those other words that people use for racial, gender and economic characterization?

On the other side of the country, words caused yet another stir after a San Francisco newspaper hailing itself as "the voice of Asian America" printed a column titled, *Why I Hate Blacks*." The writer outlined, in detail, why he supported discriminatory actions against blacks. His words simply expressed how he felt, even if others looked upon them as wrong. Of course, the paper apologized for running the column and sought the comfort and approval of the NAACP to ease its embarrassment, as most offenders of African-Americans do.

Then, there is the "G" word. Not necessarily looked upon as bad, but its varying interpretations are getting a negative nod from the gay and lesbian community. Not that gay is a bad word, but its misuse is becoming such as young people use it synonymously with stupid, dumb or silly. Happy is not an option anymore.

It is almost impossible to create and maintain a universal language with cross-cultural interpretation. Words take shape based on the intent and understanding of the user and recipient, both of whom have a right to speak their minds. Compliment? Slur? Insult? Endearment? The meaning and interpretation should be considered before words are spoken or written, because until those definitions mean the same for and to everyone, each and every word is potentially offensive to someone, somewhere. And, the First Amendment approves.

## TRUTH UNDEFINED

The Law. The Bible. Each of these embodies the opportunity and right for all to see, argue and assume a perspective on the contents that lend themselves to a particular platform or position. Their meaning left to interpretation.

Time and technology have now added another component to that which is left to understanding and question: the media. I recently received a letter from a white male media person. In the email, he outlined and validated opinions about the media and their perspective and relationship with Detroit and Detroiters. He confirmed that the media, especially the papers, didn't see Detroit as its audience and that as an organization held negative opinions of Detroiters which were easily perpetuated by their representative's geographic and social disconnect from the city and its people.

I shared this email, but not its source, on the radio show. It prompted spirited discussion that teetered between Conspiracy and cover-up. It also resulted in an email from a listener who shared a quote from John Swinton, a former writer with *The New York Times* who questioned the ability of journalists to be candid and objective in their works. He said, in part, while being feted by his fellow journalists in the 1890's that, *"There is no such thing, at this date of the world's history, in America, as an independent press. You know it and I know it. There is not one of you who dare to write your honest opinions, and if you did, you know beforehand that it would never appear in print. The business of the journalist is to destroy the truth, to lie outright, to pervert, to vilify, to fawn at the feet of mammon, and to sell his country and his race for his daily bread. You know it and I know it, and what folly is this toasting an independent press? We are the tools and vessels of rich men behind the scenes. We are the jumping jacks, they pull the strings and we dance. Our talents, our possibilities and our lives are all the property of other men."*

Ironically, I also received a link to a news video on a unrelated matter that continued to substantiate the myriad of perspectives and beliefs about what we read, hear and see, or not. The video was about the proposed North American Union and its one rule economy, and the emergence of the V-Chip. The narrator indicated that the reason why only one journalist dared talk about the unannounced and unregulated NAU was that the people behind the agreement are the same people behind mainstream media, and they don't tell you what they don't want you to know.

It is therefore an individual determination as to whether what we hear, see or read takes us one step closer to being a conscious and informed public or one separated and distracted by information otherwise disguised.

# Chapter Two:
## *Issues~Social & Otherwise*

*I once had a poster hanging in my office that read,
"Got Issues?"*

*It was there to serve as a reminder to everyone
who saw it that we all have issues—personal, professional, social, and those yet to be named.*

*Our issues-individually and collectively—can bind
us together, or ban us from our most important
source of solutions to our challenges—each other.*

# THE LEARNING TREE

Trees represent life and growth. They have roots, which ground them and hold them steady during inclement weather, and branches from which life and beauty emerge. At one time, trees also represented death and hatred, as they were the sources from which many were hanged, for nothing more than the color of their skin.

Ironically, it is a tree that is at the center of what is turning out to be one of the most racially charged incidents in a long time. Tucked away on the grounds of Jena High School in Jena, Louisiana, was a tree once reserved, if not by rule by practice, for the white students at the school. Six African-American students dared take a seat under the tree. What resulted was nothing more than a high school brawl, fueled by racial tensions, unequal access and historical injustices, as validated by nooses that were hung from the tree, and the encounter between the students that followed.

The charges, however, were as unequal as the opportunities in this small southern town of 3,000. While the white students involved in the brawl were suspended for a few days from school, the African-Americans were charged with crimes, including attempted second-degree murder. One defendant remains in jail, and is brought to visitors in ankle and wrist shackles.

I can only imagine that this same tree at one time was used to hang African-Americans, young and unsuspecting like those who one day decided to sit under this tree. I imagine, too, that this same tree offered shade to those white students of Jena High who knew and enjoyed the luxury of being able to sit under the tree without incident.

What this tree represents, or at least can be seen as, now is the opportunity for two things: for America to realistically see itself and its racial inequalities and as an opportunity for true change.

People in this country who have never been penalized or ostracized because of the color of their skin are unable or unwilling to believe that it happens everyday, or sympathize with those it happens to. For anyone who questions such, Jena is the perfect example of the challenges that America still faces. Jena also presents the perfect opportunity for a significant first step in racial resolve.

As the world watches Jena and the legal entanglements as they unfold, Jena is the microcosm of race in America. Racism, like the tree, has strong roots that have helped it to withstand the test of time and opposition; Justice can be what evolves from the otherwise tainted branches of this American injustice.

The tree in Jena has since been chopped down, and the only thing that remains is a stump. But, removing the symbols of racism are a waste of time and a slap in the face of all who seek justice if the principles and practices, like the tree stump, remain.

## ERACISM

I saw the word ERACISM on a license plate once, and thought how ingenious. A self-made word that I interpreted to mean, "erase racism." I tucked it in the back of my mind, but always quietly wondered if doing so would ever be possible. I had to pull it out and dust it off recently while listening to comments about this city and Detroiters from people who share neither of these traits.

If you ever really listen to people talk, they will tell you what they are trying not to say, like how they really feel. You will hear traces of prejudice and racism laced throughout their condescending remarks. The scary part is that most don't feel as though there is anything wrong with their negative and prejudicial perspective. What they think is wrong is that you fail to see things their way. Therein lies the problem.

We are each made of our own experiences and exposures, which make up our personalities and perspectives. These things shape who we are and how we see others and ourselves. What we fail to realize or acknowledge is that each experience is different, thereby making each of our perspectives, like us, equally varied.

It seems almost criminal and sacrilegious that we continue to harbor racist views and opinions of others who are different than we are. And, we are all guilty. We just won't admit it. We think and make collective conclusions about those of other racial and economic backgrounds. But, these are the comments we make to those who we already know or expect to share those opinions.

There is no comfort in public acknowledgment of our multiplicity of views of others. So, we pretend that they don't exist. Yet, circumstances and loose or heated discussions allow those true feeling to permeate even the safest of conversations.

If, after all of this time, we are ever to make real strides in dealing with racial injustice and views, we must first admit our true feelings and perspectives. We must openly acknowledge that we think certain things about those we probably know very little about. We must divulge our deepest thoughts and fears then recognize where those views originated. Was it television, a news story, one limited encounter, or the opinions or so-called lesson from another?

It's really sad, if nothing else, that in spite of our technological advances, educational excellence, political strides, and business savvy, that we still cannot have the simplest of honest conversations about the one thing that we must encounter on a regular basis—each other. Until we do, we will never ERACISM.

## TAKE NOTE, LESSONS FROM THE LIFE AND DEATH OF EMMIT TILL

I recently watched a documentary on PBS about Emmit Till, a 14-year-old young black man who, in 1955, was killed by two white men for allegedly whistling at a white woman. It was a moving and compelling story that in no way can be reproduced on these pages (visit www.pbs.org). And, in this documentary, I found so many lessons that I felt should drive not just Black History month, but should be the very basis of black existence all year long.

The first lesson I got was when one of Mississippi's white residents was commenting on the arrest and trial of the two white men who killed Mr. Till. (I say killed and not accused because just four months after they were acquitted of his murder, they sold their story to

LOOK Magazine for $4,000, and admitted their criminal act.) He said that they looked upon these two men *with the same disdain we do blacks, but the bottom line is that they are still white.* He said this in response to the overwhelming support that was shown to these two men. They were poor, came from nothing and had even less. That which some may even call "poor white trash.' They were bottom of the barrel...so much so that they put them on the level with blacks...but they were still white. That was enough to offer unconditional support. Take note.

The second lesson was when two men who had actually witnessed Mr. Till's kidnapping, and heard his cries came forward to testify in the sweltering heat and hate of Mississippi in the 1950's. But, while they knew speaking out jeopardized their lives, they felt that not speaking out was an even greater jeopardy. And, while they had to leave the south for northern safety after their testimony, they spoke out just the same. Take another note.

Justice did not serve the late Mr. Till or his family any justice, having acquitted these two murderers without much consideration. One of the jurors even commented that it would not have taken them the twenty minutes that it did to reach a decision if they had not paused for a drink of pop. The times did not allow for many—if any—alternatives to this decision. After the men sold their story and admitted how they killed the young Mr. Till, his mother sought to have federal intervention and reopen the case. But, even President Eisenhower and J. Edgar Hoover said "no." So, what is a black, seemingly powerless but obviously violated, family to do?

Well, the two white men owned a store. The store's main customer base was black. So, the blacks in the small, white and racist town quietly but effectively boycotted the store, running it out of business as a result.

A dramatic occurrence, with three distinct and time transcending messages: stick together, regardless. If the other person looks like you, that should be enough to support them, respect them and acknowledge your kinship. Secondly, speak up for what is right.

In a day when we face so many challenges, and so many people hold close their ideas and information that could very well make things better, please speak up. Don't fear the repercussions of speaking up because the greater danger is in keeping silent. And last but not least--learn and pay attention to the power of your money, people. It has a power—like you individually and we collectively-- far greater than you imagine or want to acknowledge.

## YOU CANNOT REGULATE
## MORALITY

The issue of the moment seems to be proposed adult entertainment venues that are seeking to locate in the city of Detroit. As businesses, they want to come into, take part and contribute to the vibrancy now evident in the city; they want to pay taxes and redevelop otherwise stagnant and abandoned properties and vacant land. And, they want to do so under existing laws and zoning regulations set forth by the city. Bottom line, they want to do business.

On the other hand, there are community and religious leaders who are up in arms about the nature of these proposed establishments. They are citing immorality, and the alleged contribution to the degradation of the family and society if these businesses open up. Hold on, everybody. The city will go to hell in a hand basket if "these places" open.

Well, the pendulum of freedom swings both ways. Freedom that exists in this city and country allows for individuals to make choices made available to them by those same freedoms. If adult entertainment is an available option, then it remains just that, an option. Removing this as a choice does not make one more moral or righteous than one would be if they chose to patronize such an establishment. Don't like them? Then, don't go. No one is holding a gun, using coercion or blackmail to make people patronize these places. But, the truth is, these establishments make an unbelievable amount of money. Somebody has to agree with the entertainment offered, because the patronage is quite profitable. While I respect those who are taking time and spending money to fight these proposed businesses, I cannot help but to feel that their resources would be better served in areas that have a greater and more positive impact on the people whose interest they say they are protecting. I would be more sensitive to their position if, say, they shouted equally as loud about education and health care. Where are those voices on these issues?

Perhaps if the goal is to remove all things that have a negative influence and impact on the community, then the list is missing a ton of other things clearly more damaging, such as drugs, cigarettes, alcohol, fast foods, child abuse, violence—domestic and otherwise--and the list then becomes endless. What about the casinos, lottery, R-rated movies, rap music, music videos, and loud and offensive behavior? These, too, are things in which people voluntarily engage. Why are these opposing efforts selective? What makes this different than anything else that can be looked upon as less than ideal? Where does it end? It doesn't.

In a perfect world, things would be just that. Perfect. But, they are not. People would speak what they really feel, and their opposition or support of something would and could be taken at face value, without the possibility of a hidden agenda. It has been whispered to me that there is something more than meets the eye behind the protest, perhaps it's for show to the shouters constituents, could be the money, or the fact that an outlet will exist that they cannot publicly patronize. Who knows? Personally, who cares?

There are a lot of things that exist in this country that don't meet with blanket approval—certain religions, homosexuality, gambling, even pork as a meal choice. If those things do not hurt or impose on the rights of others, then it all boils down to personal choice, which is the right of each and every person in this country.

Many are already too preoccupied with the preference and practice of others—what and who they like, what they do or don't do, what they wear and how they wear it. If we would each focus our efforts on our own personal practices and behaviors, and quit trying to regulate those of others, we would all truly be better off. Therein lies many of our problems, trying to make others like us.

This issue also begs of a larger question—what is moral, and who here is justified in making approval of that which is or is not so? Who are we to pass judgment on others? We aren't, and those who are doing so need to quit. Focus on the real issues that strangle our communities every day, not that which people have a right to choose, or deny.

When the perimeters of freedom allow for that which some do not approve, those perimeters cannot be moved and altered as circumstance and personal demand dictate. Life is a lot simpler when we realize and accept that you choose and patronize that which you like, and bypass that which you do not.

# ILLITERACY DERSERVES SOLUTION

In every conversation or discussion about the challenges we face in this city and surrounding area, the excuse for the offenders is always because "they just don't know any better." This reason is applied for the gamut of community and self-destructive behaviors, from committing crimes to throwing trash in the streets. The sad reality is that too many people don't know any better, and ignorance continues to fuel our community's downward spiral.

While Pro-Literacy, under the direction of Margaret Williamson, is certainly doing its part the problem is daunting. With an illiteracy rate of more than 47% and growing in the city alone, the problem cannot be tackled by one entity. That means that 1 out of nearly every 3 people you encounter is unable to read. Research unquestionably supports the fact that being able to read is crucial to both survival and being able to contribute to one's home and community. And yet, no research is needed to validate its importance to how people behave and respond.

Not being able to read is a form of mental incarceration that prevents one from ever realizing or enjoying life. It is also a source of frustration that can lead to destructive behavior, and puts those who cannot read at the bottom of the social and economic barrel.

Reading is like the true sixth sense, as it allows for a freedom of expression, control and the ability to make choices and decisions that shape a life and destiny. We can look around and see the negative impact of students who have been allowed to pass through school without the proper reading abilities. It should rightfully be looked upon as a social ill.

Other major cities have campaigns and initiatives fueled by comprehensive partnerships between those who realize the social and economic effect that illiteracy can have on a city and its residents. With Detroit being home to one of the highest illiteracy rates in the United States, I have to ask where is ours?

Organizations, groups and individuals often use their respective platforms to complain about issues they feel are important. Yet, I wonder where is the proactive and responsible call to action to help eradicate our citizen's inability to read? Why is it that no one sees, or will admit to seeing the tsunami-like impact that illiteracy is having on our city?

Reading is a right. But, it is also a responsibility, one that should be—must be—assumed by every person who has any interest in this city and its people. More importantly, all will benefit from its eradication. Employers, residents, community activists, political and religious leaders, media outlets, retail and entertainment venues and cultural institutions are all impacted by our illiteracy ratio, as is our crime and unemployment rate, tolerance level and true ability to grow.

# Chapter Three:
## *Education*

*Education is the key...to everything. It provides access to survival, livelihood, quality of life and happiness. It is the keeper of success, and all of the fruits therein.*

*Yet, in spite of its proven value, education remains undervalued and trivialized in urban communities across America.*

*An apathetic approach, selective support, and limited resources place these students in a compromised position.*

*When, and how, will we ever "get it?"*

# DON'T GET CAUGHT HOLDING THE SIGN

June is fast approaching, and graduations and matriculations are plentiful. During these transitional times, those moving ahead seek messages of inspiration and encouragement to continue their journey. Well, I have one to add: Don't get caught holding the sign. And, there are two signs to avoid.

All over the metropolitan area, you see people standing on street corners holding signs for companies, promoting their services or goods. From cell phones to pizzas to anything else for sale, there is a sign telling you about it, and a person holding that sign. These designated sign-holders are there regardless of the weather, and endure both the stares from the curious and being ignored by the disinterested. Now, on one hand, this may be a great first job for some, or even a part-time job for others. The key is being able to choose holding the sign, rather than being forced to for lack of options.

This is not a job that requires much skill, thought or preparation. You stand there and hold a sign, period. I doubt if a degree or previous experience is required, or if the pay will accelerate you into early retirement. So, if this is the only job for which you qualify, then you made a wrong turn someplace. Sure, this is honest and legal, but certainly not something that anyone should be forced to do, if avoidable.

The other sign is usually of the handmade kind. Written on cardboard or any other writable surface, with the assistance of crayon, marker, pencil or pen. It holds a message of request, asking for food or money, though not specifically. Rather, it summarizes ones current condition: unemployed, homeless, hungry, or the like. Its goal is to incite sympathy, and a donation of sort from the reader. While there are some who use this as an opportunity to hustle the kind-hearted, the unfortunate reality is that this is what some have been reduced to in order to survive.

These are the signs of the times, and are stark realities that should serve as in inspiration for those who are now at the threshold of their careers, educational or professional. While circumstances and life's curves are unforeseen and cannot be predicted, it is in the best interest of all who can do so, to prepare as much as possible to prevent being the holders of either of these signs.

Those who can make a difference should now do so. They should view these signs as avoidable, and work hard to keep them that way. At the same time, they should con-sider the holders of these signs as beacons of a message that should ring loud and clear to all: life awaits you with all of its uncertainty and elusiveness. Sure, it holds great things for those who are able to grasp them. But for those who cannot, the signs are not promising.

## LEARNING SHOULD BE INCENTIVE ENOUGH

Last week was the day that counted, or rather the day that students in each school district were counted by State offi-cials. The tallies are used to determine 80 percent of the funding received by each district from the state. With a minimum price tag of $6,700 on the head of each student, there was a lot at stake. So, for the Detroit District, which continues its effort to place their students at the top of the list, one hundred percent attendance was necessary. So, bring out the bells, whistles, prizes and incentives to get the students to school, their parents to bring them, and to put on what translates to me as nothing more than a game face for the day.

I found the whole concept of enticing parents and kids to come in the count to be a bit exploitative. I will give you a prize if you come to school today. Well, what about yesterday, and more importantly what about tomorrow? I am struggling to understand the importance of getting the kids there today for the sole purpose of insuring that the district receives money for those kids. This is money that is supposed to enhance their education as well as their academic preparedness. District scores indicate otherwise.

Now, in all fairness, credit must be given for what I interpret as an aggressive approach by then Superintendent Kenneth Burnley to reiterate the basics, especially reading. That alone is admirable, and the results are surely to be positive and evident at some point. Overall, however, there is much that needs to be done. But, perhaps the reading emphasis is as good of a place as any to start.

Regardless, I have a real issue with this get-them-in-for-one-day mentality and behavior.

School and the education obtained as a result of attending should be—simply because it is—marketed as the sole reward. Putting pleasure in the form of gifts and prizes before the very principle of learning is a dangerous thing. It sends the wrong message that the kids only matter when they're counted.

A day of fun, celebrities, incentives and compromised school work is no way to teach kids about the importance of school and instill a solid value of its worth. So, the day is not as appealing because the ice cream is gone, the celebrities are not there and the books have been reopened. Gee, that's no fun. But, who says that school is supposed to be?

A comfortable environment should be created to encourage attendance and learning on a regular basis. African-Americans, especially, should loudly tout the value of education, as well as their historical struggle for education. Maybe with this, we will begin to repair the damaged and compromised view of education that many of our children, and some of their parents, hold.

Going to school should be promoted on a regular and on-going basis for the self-investment that it is. It is the means to an end, and a road that must be traveled if one is to ever really "get anywhere." It is not nor should be communicated as the place for prizes, fun and games for the one day a year when there is a bounty on the heads of students. This is selective interest, paid concern, and nothing more than pimping at its best.

## LET'S ALL GO BACK TO SCHOOL

As children of all ages prepare to return to school, it is an opportunity for everyone to take part in what can be an academic and social victory for all. While buying pencils and backpacks are important, it is time for all to rethink our roles and contributions to the success of our students, and society.

First and foremost, parents can establish an environment conducive to learning. This begins with the conversation and tone set when talking about school, teachers, homework and preparation. If and when parents assume a negative approach and outlook towards school, the children will assume the same.

Parents can make an early connection with and commitment to a partnership with the teachers and school. Meet the teachers, attend meetings, visit the school and offer to volunteer or contribute to the school's efforts, if possible and when necessary. This sets the positive tone that the teachers and school can count on the parent for contributions to the student's academic achievements.

Everyone must understand and embrace the increasing importance of education. We must see and acknowledge how education, or the lack thereof, shapes lives and impacts the world in which we live. Somewhere along the line, that connection has been dropped.

On the larger scale, the community at-large must embrace all of our students at every level. Those working within the school systems must recommit to their jobs and role in educating the students. Those representing the interests of our students and the community must also remind themselves and the community of their roles and responsibilities, as well as their efforts—failures and accomplishments included.

Even those without biological children have a role and responsibility, as students one day will become those encountered in business, politics or on the street. Those educated, or not, today will run the world, or the streets, tomorrow.

Personalities and politics aside, it is time to place education at the top of everyone's list. It is a priority that must be infused into every action by everyone—elected officials, parents, teachers, students, corporations, the media, and all in between.

It's past time to reevaluate what we have done and have been doing without thought or alteration of action. Rote education is a thing of the past. We need innovation and proactive involvement from all levels.

The school year always represents a fresh start, a new beginning for students. It's a time to start over, break bad habits, develop positive ones, and get on the right track. Let's let this school year represent the same for everyone else, as well.

# CELEBRATE EXCELLENCE NOT NORMALCY

June is the month for graduations, when students move from one level of education and expectations to another. It is also a time of exaggerated and unjustified affairs that mark the passing of students from one grade to another. In spite of what many believe and celebrate, passing from kindergarten to first grade is not call for a major social event.

Not just across town, but also all over the country, urban areas are plagued with the unnecessary and misleading practices of over-celebrating what should otherwise be looked upon and responded to as normal. Limousines, tuxedos, lavish parties and the like are becoming the tools of tradition to mark what should otherwise garner a congratulatory word and guidance for the rest of the journey.

The wrong message is being sent to those who are doing nothing more than passing, and in some sad cases simply being passed along. Doing what one is *supposed* to do is not cause for celebration. Sure, positive affirmation and reassurance given to those who are moving in the right direction are good and can't hurt. But, exaggerated commemoration is dangerous.

This sends the signal that normalcy and meeting minimal expectations are what bring about lavish rewards. Not so. It is excellence that will, and should, reap higher returns. Certainly with so many students dropping out shortly after middle school, you can't help but to give thanks for those who make it every step of the way.

Yet, rather than waste resources, including time and money, on empty and uninspiring festivities to celebrate what should otherwise be expected, the focus should drastically shift to raising the level of expectations. We should not expect or celebrate a 2.0 grade point average, because that is exactly what that is—*average*. And, there is nothing great about a student who attends school on a regular basis. It's a requirement. They are *supposed* to be there every day.

As we watch failure become more and more acceptable throughout society, it is time to step up the game. Global competitiveness extends beyond the boundaries of one's neighborhood and city limits. Options are now restricted to two—success or failure. There is no longer a gray area, once known as the middle class. One either prepares and succeeds, or doesn't prepare and fails.

It is time to shift from our apparent contentment with mediocrity. We must progress to and appropriately celebrate a level of excellence that reflects the true meaning of such— superiority, distinction and quality. It's long past time that we make this move, and we don't need to rent a limousine to get there.

# YALE VS YOU TUBE

In an era of immediate everything—responses, returns and gratification, the battle between long-term planning for a solid future is in a full-battle with instant success. From Soldier Boy to disgruntled divorcees, the Internet and electronic options for self-promotion and success are becoming viable options for those seeking a new form of success: the instant kind.

Efforts like those of JoAnn Wolf and City Prep are diligently trying to introduce Ivy League schools as options for kids who might not otherwise be exposed; on the pretense that higher-level education offers a unique chance at privileged access. Here lies the true American Dream of achieving an education on the grounds where ideas are born, and industries fueled.

On the other end of the continuum, there lies the likes of You-Tube, where everyone is already a star, a success in their own pre-determined right and no education required. Here, creativity is the driving force and success measured by sheer number of hits. Marketing is done by word of mouth, FaceBook® and the relentless emailing of links to the video that you've "got to see."

It makes me wonder if bragging rights, once limited to university and college affiliations, and shown by school colors and alum contributions, are now being replaced by the number of views and hits on a site or link. How many do you have?

Everyone wants to be successful. And, once upon a time, success was defined by the sheer effort that went into the outcome. It was the story being made to tell once you arrived at the top of your chosen game. How much practice?

How many failures? These were all indications of the perseverance that helped to make success that much sweeter.

The challenge used to be convincing students that "professional athlete" was not a dependable career option, and selling them on at least a more viable alternative. Now, options are abundant and require minimal skill. Silliness, satire, comedy and just plain stupidity all occupy the plans that once were centered on education.

Schools no longer have to compete with each other for students as much as schools now have to collectively compete against Internet options of immediate celebrity. Sure, it's fun and even funny to peek into the lives of suburban women trying to do the Soldier Boy, or the cute baby giving the camera an evil eye, and the Mad TV skit of Bon Qui Qui at King Burger.

While this is fun, and even profitable for those whose careers have taken off as a result, it's no replacement for hard work and success. Nor does it fill the void for the recognition that comes from being the best of the best rather than simply being the one with the most You Tube views.

# Chapter Four:
## *Culture*

*Our culture. It is who we are, what we do, and how we do it. It has been cause for criticism, and celebration.*

*But, for whatever it is worth, it is the fabric of our being and deserves recognition and respect, from others…and us.*

# RAP'S BAD REP

I have been a fan of rap music since its inception, back in the days of Curtis Blow, LL Cool J and Run DMC. I even appreciated the power of the lyrical word back to rap's origination, and the days of the Last Poets. They reminded us all "the revolution would not be televised." Like it or not, Rap is an art form, and both enjoys the freedom of expression and the penalty of personal preference.

In time, I have watched—or heard—rap music evolve from a projected fly-by-night fad into a multi-billion dollar phenomenon that has infiltrated every aspect of American being.

From rap has emerged a culture, dubbed hip-hop. It is revered, and reviled—a compilation of contradiction. Whatever it is or considered to be, one thing is for sure—it is here to stay.

This week, there were many people upset about the upcoming Hip-Hop Summit announcement. The words tossed around were something about these rappers being poor role models and promoters of violence and all things bad. "Don't bring these people to my school," they shouted. "Not for my kids," they demanded.

Well, I invite a closer look at the rap game. Or, in the words of MC Serch, "It's not a game." The issue here is not whether these successful entertainers are bad role models, the heart of the issue is the simple ability of some to get the emotional goose of others.

The first reality here is that these people are entertainers. What they do is perform for the purpose of entertaining others. While the method of some may be unorthodox, I pose the question of whether art imitates life or vice versa. Then, there is the side to rap that many fail or choose not to see--the business side. Many rappers have made the transition into acting and producing other artists, which opens the doors for others to follow. There are clothing lines and restaurants. For Rapper Jay-Z, there is even a Vodka distribution company in Russia. These are sound business decisions that elevate young black men and women—who may otherwise not be productive contributors to society—to another economic level. But, we have to see this for what it is—a business.

There are also the quiet contributions that many rappers make to community and social efforts. I promised that I would not reveal the name, but one rapper who was under fire in this recent attack quietly wrote a check last year for $50,000 to help make sure that the efforts of one of our local radio stations could fulfill its holiday community commitment. No cameras, no media. Just contributions for the good of many who now, unknowingly, criticize their supporter.

Another issue that I have is with criticism of lyrical content. Yes, some of it is a bit much.

Rather, too much, to be honest. But, it rivals what I overhear in local malls and grocery stores from average people. The difference is that listening to the music is a choice. The label indicates if the lyrics warrant serious consideration, or the choice exists to buy—as I often do—the edited versions of the same CD's.

More importantly, though, is the role model matter. Parents must do a couple of things—they must first stop looking to public figures to raise or influence their children. A parent is a child's first and strongest influence. If that power is in place, then exterior attempts to sway the child are failed efforts. Secondly, they must recognize and teach the difference between entertainment and reality. My children know that what they see on television, play on their video games or hear on the radio or CD's is for the sole purpose of entertainment; they know that the underlying goal of entertainment is to make money; and that they do not duplicate what they see or hear. They know this because my husband and I talk to them about it every chance we get. Not preaching to them, but in conversation when the opportunity arises, which is often.

Most importantly, as avid listeners of all kinds of music, including rap, we serve as examples to our children. They watch and listen to us more closely than any rapper or television figure. They realize that they have minds of their own, enjoy the freedom of speech and ability to enjoy that which is available to them in this country, as well as the freedom of choice to choose something other than that which they do not enjoy.

A rapper or even ex-convict coming to a school is hardly reason for the madness, especially when there are more real and serious issues on the burner.

Disappointingly, most people weren't even clear about what they were upset about. They were simply being what they obviously fear that their children are or will become— uninformed followers.

## ONE BAD APPLE CAN SPOIL THE WHOLE BUNCH

The old saying goes that "one bad apple does not spoil the

whole bunch." Yet, when I picked up the paper recently to see that a 17-year old Detroiter was arrested for the murder of two of his former co-workers at a new downtown eatery, I knew otherwise.

Beyond the apparent tragedy of this senseless situation lies other deep and far reaching implications. This man carries the weight and paints a picture of other young men, other black men, and Detroit, at-large. At a time when we as a city are witnessing small but steady and significant gains, something like this is more than a setback. I can hear the kitchen table conversations, laced with racial and geographic stereotypes that are further fueled by this one man's actions. He is the face that is feared by people who have shunned this city and written it off as dead; he's the face that many elders look down upon, shaking their heads at his foolishness of youth; he is the face that others see in the eyes of every other black person that they encounter. To many, he is us, and we are him.

When businesses want to locate in the city, Councilwoman JoAnn Watson is relentless in asking about and ensuring the involvement and employment of Detroiters in the process. Why? While everyone does not respond in such an embarrassingly ignorant manner, this man's action makes the argument more difficult if not impossible because "his" actions define how "they" all act.

Certainly, there are disgruntled employees of all races in every corner of the country that have responded in violent and senseless manners. Yet, Detroit cannot afford to act like everyone else. We have come too far, and have too much to gain to risk being like everyone else. We don't have the luxury of a margin of error to participate in foolishness.

We have a local sports figure who decides to invest in the home city of his team. It is one of many attractions in a downtown that has not resembled such in years. People are visiting, moving in, walking around, albeit gingerly, and beginning to rediscover a city that has fought a bad rap for far too long.

Detroit has long been the stepchild of the region, the country. Never allowed growing pains or public puberty, it has always been all or nothing. When every piece of blowing paper makes the city a garbage dump, every ousted streetlight equates to a blackout, every accident is a catastrophe and every mishap a setback, every single person that lives here needs to understand that and act accordingly. Their hiccups are our heart attacks.

Fair or not, it is time to stop the stupidity. Until we surpass our goals, and maybe not even then, each of our actions as Detroiters will represent everyone else that shares a characteristic—age, race, religion or residency. We should all accept that, and act accordingly.

## R.I.P. SHOULD MEAN JUST THAT

In a period of one week, three internationally recognized figures were laid to rest. Well, sort of. The deaths of former President Gerald Ford, Soul Legend James Brown and displaced Iraqi leader, Saddam Hussein, were as varied as their lives.

For eight days, former President Ford was carted around the country so those who reveled in his legacy—real or perceived—could pay their final respects. From Washington, DC, to California to Grand Rapids, Michigan, his remains—and that is what they were—clocked frequent flier miles for more than a week. Enough already.

For former Iraqi President, Saddam Hussein, it took less than the time it took Gerald Ford to make his final rounds for him to be tried, convicted and hanged, only to then have the United Nations question whether or not the process was fair and correct. A little late, don't you think? No long ceremony or celebration. Only a black suit, matching scarf, a noose, no hood, mind you, and then bootleg video of the hanging on the Internet was all that marked the end of his days.

Then, there was "Soul Brother Number One"—James Brown. A horse drawn carriage took him on his final ride through the streets of Harlem to the chants and cheers of his throngs of fans as he made his final trek to the performance venue of black stars everywhere—the famed Apollo Theater. There, under the constant guard of the Reverend Al Sharpton—don't ask me why—he lay for all to see and marvel if not at his career, then at least at his purple satin suit, one of three outfits he wore during his public viewing. Then, off to his home state of South Carolina, where at the writing of this column, he lay—days after his official funeral-- locked in his home while his wife and children wrangle over his estate and where his final resting place should be.

Paying final respects should not last as long as the life of the deceased. We are seeing this increasing practice with those whose lives we choose to celebrate upon their death. But celebrating and exploiting are two different things, and the lines should not be marred. Where are the days that people traveled to the city or state of the final service? If there were unable to make it, they shared in the service in spirit and good memories of the deceased. Funerals should not be traveling shows, endless opportunities for the showmanship of others, or be-

...come video fodder for YouTube®.

I watched during this week of varying yet equally ostentatious display of finality, shaking my head. When we wish those who have gone before us—regardless of how or why-- to "rest in peace," then we should sincerely allow them to do so.

## TELEVISION: The New Crack

I remember the 80's when the influx of crack cocaine seemed to permeate every aspect of American urban communities. If you didn't smoke crack, you knew someone that did, or you knew someone that sold it. If you missed any of these categories, you could simply look around and see the impact that its effect was having on our community. If you didn't see it then, it was evident later when the offspring of those addicted were born, creating another layer of problems with which we were forced to deal.

Well, the 80's are gone, and the drug trade seems to hum along without the fanfare that it did back then. But, look a little closer and you see its replacement. It has the same intensity, and apparent addiction. Yet, the numbers are higher, and the potential negative impact event greater. You don't have to sneak and buy it, and no one looks down on you socially for partaking. As a matter of fact, users try to get the biggest and most expensive brands, touting is as a status symbol regardless of his harmful effects. The dealers are licensed, and accept money openly in public. They are allowed to charge taxes, and even permitted to advertise their product. People come and buy in droves, and the addiction is fueled and in full swing.

The effects are staggering. People sit in a vegetative state observing, wallowing in their damaging pleasure. The statistics of children impacted by this new drug are growing at an alarming rate, while people young and old struggle with its only know vaccine—reading and exercising. Using this new drug requires no thought or physical activity, other than the minimal use of ones fingers to bring forth the variety it offers.

This new drug alone has created an entire population of zombie-like creatures who are nothing less than addicted. Yes, addicted. Children and adults alike can recite the programming of any given channel far faster than their multiplication tables or professional statistics for their jobs. From children's cartoons, to sports-only channels to dramas and violence-laden shows, everyone has their preferred form of this new drug.

But, I refuse to be a part of the masses that are set-forth on this path of irreversible destruction. As I watched my children argue over whose turn it was to watch the largest television in the house, they reminded me of crack-addicts. That's it, I thought. So, away went all of the televisions. Let them be someone else's problem. From the largest to the smallest, the televisions are no more. Better yet, we cancelled the cable. No more $100 a month habits. There is really something more, and better to do.

This was a strong but firm decision that my husband and I made, and have stuck to thus far, to make sure that our children want and do more than learn to change channels. Life is not quite that simple. It sometimes actually requires thought and action. No better way to prepare them, than to take action ourselves.

Television entertainment can be a good thing, but sometimes too much of anything can be bad. The statistics are over-whelming. And, while literacy levels fall, and obesity levels rise, we all better take a good and hard look at ourselves.

We did, and didn't even have to attend any rehabilitation meetings.

## CHANGING THE COMPLEXION OF CLASSICAL MUSIC

People of color represent less than 4% of those in classical music. While this statistic is disappointing, it may not come as a shock to many. After all, classical music is not the genre normally associated with African-Americans and La-tinos, but it should be. At least that is what Aaron Dworkin believes, and is working hard to make a reality.

As founder and President of the Sphinx Organization, Dworkin has labored long and hard to change the face, and ears, of classical music. Sphinx is dedicated to encouraging and supporting the presence and performances of African – Americans and Latinos in classical music. Through several initiatives and with offices in Detroit and Harlem, Sphinx is providing the opportunity for people of color to play with and inspire others who look like them.

Driven by his own feeling of alienation as the lone African-American violin player as a child, Dworkin realized that he didn't like the feeling of being the "only one." A classical violinist, Dworkin knew of the historical presence of Afri-can-Americans in classical music. From Jose Mauricio Nunes Garcia to Le Chevalier de Saint Georges, classical music has long had a colorful but oft unknown presence.

Today, the numbers are growing due in part to the efforts of Dworkin and his team as they continue to travel around the country introducing and engaging people of color in classical music. By teaching and training at an early age, Sphinx is creating a talented reservoir of people of color from which orchestras and symphonies all around the world can choose. Additionally, Sphinx has its own Symphony Orchestra in which many laureates and Sphinx Competition winners go on to perform.

In addition to changing the color of on-stage presence, these efforts are paying off in terms of altering the audience, as well. Having a friend, family member or neighbor perform is a reason for many to first venture into orchestral halls and classical performances. Many find themselves intrigued and impressed, and eager to return. What was once viewed as highbrow and off-limits is now a viable educational and entertainment option for all.

Dworkin and Sphinx recognized early the value of exposure to classical music. It, like other things, can alter one's perception of others, and themselves. In the face of increased entertainment temptations that lure our children down an undesirable path, Sphinx is a welcomed option as they change the face and complexion of classical music-- one performer, one audience member at a time.

# Chapter Five:
## *Politics*

*Like it or not, everything is political.
And, in a city like Detroit, the political climate can be very temperamental.*

*Locally or nationally, politics can shape and sway the way we live...or die.*

*Yet, it remains the democratic outlet for a voice that was once, and would have otherwise remained, silent.*

# ALL CAMPAIGNS SHOULD BEGIN AT MACK & BEWICK

Obviously taking a page from Mayor Kwame Kilpatrick's handbook, Senator Debbie Stabenow hit the streets. Last week, while driving down Mack Avenue, I happened upon the preparation for Senator Stabenow's visit. I saw the signs, heard music and wondered what was going on. I stopped and asked what was going on, and was Senator Stabenow present. Charles Williams, a campaign coordinator, told me she was on her way. *Really?!?!*

Now, if you are not familiar, Mack and Bewick is the eastside equivalent of Dexter and Davison. It's the point that represents all of the mix represented by this city. It's the struggle, and the success; the efforts and failures all housed on one corner. It is the pulse not measured by polls and telephone surveys. It's where you find the people that sometimes feel forgotten, but who need to be heard the most.

It is also where I dare all candidates to take their messages, because it unfamiliar territory for many. And, that translates to fear. So, instead, most candidates who want to reach "the people" resort to places of worship, community centers and public picnics. The safe havens for delivering a message.

But, the last Mayoral election proved that the power indeed lies with the people, and that if you want them to support you, you have to reach out and touch them, literally. And, you can only do that by going where they go, and doing what they do. Mayor Kilpatrick has the enviable ability to relate to folks from all walks of life, of varying social and economic backgrounds with equally diverse interests. He took his Detroit experience, combined it with his formal education and made a helluva public servant. He hit the streets.

Nearly 100 people, some recognizable, others nameless, attended the gathering at Mack and Bewick for Senator Stabenow. There was ice cream—Good Humor, no less—hot dogs, music and mingling. I sat and watched the dynamics of the event, and was impressed that the Senator seemed pretty comfortable. The Tiger Lady was there, as were others who made the corner their court, which they usually hold daily. I even noted an attempt to dance made by the Senator and Reverend Horace Sheffield. Not bad, not bad at all.

There were some other elected officials, and some who hoped to be. I figured they were simply piggybacking off of her presence at a place they obviously hadn't thought of or considered visiting on their own, which reduced their street credibility in my eyes.

From now on, every person running for public office ought to go exactly and directly where their constituents are, whether it's the liquor store or corporate headquarters, the corner office or simply the corner. I really want to see and know that people, who promise to represent all, actually know who constitutes such. After all, packaged politicians only go to churches, but real public servants go to the people.

## THE PORCH IS A START

I didn't think the conversations about Mayor Kwame Kilpatrick's comments—suggesting that people get off of their porches, and passing the drug tests for jobs- would last this long, but surprisingly they have.

There are those who insist on making his comments into something negative, rather than accepting them for the call to action that I interpreted them to be. I have long said two things: that people should get off of their porches to see for themselves what is going on, rather than leave their impressions and perceptions to others who know equally as little or less, and that the Mayor is the only elected official that I hear saying what needs to be said rather than placating his consistency.

The porch, to me, represents the place where people sit and watch what is happening around them. They make comments about those they see, and draw conclusions about that which they can't see all while perched on a place that does not encourage engagement.

For too many, the porch is a safe haven from reality. When things look bad from the stoop, one can retreat inside, blind from the truths that present themselves to onlookers. The porch represents that area of apprehension and reservation, rather than one of involvement and contribution. It could have just as well been an easy chair, couch or the basement. The point is that it's a place of inactivity.

So, while those who are sitting on the porch, literally or figuratively, watching and waiting for something to happen, opportunities are passing them by. For those who are smoking marijuana while waiting on the porch, jobs are passing them by and going unfilled.

People may not want to admit it, but there are several areas of industry and professions that are unable to hire many Detroiters for the simple reason of their inability to pass the drug test. Look at the police department, whose complexion has changed drastically since the days of Coleman Young, who fought for a department representative of the community it served. It's not that people are not applying; it's that they are failing the drug test, period.

Taking advantage of the job and growth opportunities that exist in this city, and there are many, means the assumption of responsibility by individuals. Jobs will not come knocking on the door looking to be filled.

Our elected officials can create endless programs and policies to help citizens, but people must be actively engaged and prepared to participate, even if that means getting off of the porch to do so.

## YES, WE CAN

Like so many others around the country, this is the first time that I have ever really paid attention to and felt involved in a presidential campaign. There is, for the first time, energy, excitement, opportunity and hope. For this, I credit Democratic candidate Barack Obama. I have been reading and watching as his campaign gains momentum, being a witness to an amazing revolution unfolding right here in America, and during Black History Month, no less.

America has long promoted itself as the land of the free, and the source of opportunity for all. Yet, the record of America has long been tarnished with less than impressive records of being either. Contradictory and hypocritical policies and practices have, over the years, made America more of a disappointment than the shining example of democracy and freedom that it alleged itself to be.

Sure, America has many advantages over other countries.

Yet, it lags behind many other countries in numerous areas, as well. We really no longer have the bragging rights to technology advantages, educational excellence, or shared wealth. Instead, we trail behind countries that use America as an opportunity for advancement of their own cultural agendas. We boast otherwise, with the right to do so long gone.

What America now has the opportunity to do through the vision and efforts of Obama is to be the country that it could have been, or even should have been long ago. As a black man makes his way through the ranks of becoming the Democratic nominee, people who have been cast aside and overlooked, now see evidence of the dream. The American Dream, and the dream that so many believe died with civil rights leader Martin Luther King, Jr.

Obama is bringing hope to a country that has seemingly for decades functioned on automatic pilot fueled by apathy, with minimal interest or intervention from the people; all of the people. He is proof to children and adults that the impossible is really doable. He's showing Americans that there are concerns and connections that transcend race, color, gender and economics. And, that it is possible to have a unified agenda that addresses seemingly varied interests.

Obama is shattering stereotypes, and establishing a new image for black men, all men, and every American equally. He is doing this because his reality is a contradiction to what so many long held on to as true.

I am excited about the Presidential election, and the opportunities and promise for this country and all therein because of the candidacy of Barack Obama. It's a time for everyone to become what they've long said they were, or wanted to be; it's a time for America to become what it was truly intended to be, for all who are here. Can it be done? Yes, it can. Can we do it? Yes, we can.

# WHEN BLACK WAS REASON ENOUGH

As the 2008 Presidential Campaign gains momentum, it also continues to highlight an increasingly confusing dilemma amongst African-Americans as some struggle with whether or not to vote for the only African-American candidate, Barack Obama. It seems that many African-Americans find it necessary to include his experience, voting record and character indicators in the equation used to determine his presidential capabilities, and to secure their vote. It seems that they want to remove the veil of color from their list of considerations, even though color was once reason enough.

It wasn't long ago when segregation was clearly evident on the books, tongues and in the practices of America. Being black was reason enough to spew hate from those who didn't welcome their presence; being black was reason enough to not be welcome at lunch counters, restrooms and water fountains; being black was reason enough not to be able to ride in the front of the bus or share a classroom with those whose skin was of a different color.

Even not so long ago, being black seemed reason enough to be excessively sentenced for crimes for which white counterparts were overlooked or gently admonished; being black is now reason to not garner serious consideration, or to simply be overlooked when applying for college, thanks to the elimination of Proposal 2 in several states around the country, and remains reason enough to be taunted with

nooses as a reminder of the past. Being black alone is reason for a lot of things, but obviously not reason enough to
support Obama.

While Obama never made race an issue, Hillary and Bill
Clinton have done so and validated Obama's blackness as
a result. This has good and bad implications, especially for
those who want to hold on to the illusion of Bill Clinton
being the, or close to, first black President of the United
States.

If an Asian, a middle easterner, and a Latino replaced
Obama's presence, those cultural groups would not sec-
ond-guess their support for his candidacy. They wouldn't
fear electing someone who might not be qualified, or
someone who may not have the country's best interest at
hand, but rather would be driven by their cultural pride and
the opportunity to elevate their visibility and political
power by electing one of their own.

Black has historically been reason enough for many things,
to many people. For black people, it's time for it, too, to be
reason enough.


# THE SIMPLICITY OF SUCCESS

Leaders from southeast Michigan gather once again at
Mackinac to assess and strategize about how to overcome
social, economic and educational challenges in the region.
Yet, I am reminded of the true meaning of success: making
a difference.

Making a difference is not always found in a policy paper,
law or plan of action. Rather, it is what we decide to do
when we encounter an opportunity to make a change, for

others and ourselves.

Success has long being presented in the package of big title, corner office and at least a six-figure salary. It has long meant name recognition and power brokering for the benefit of a bottom line. But, as we look around communities all across the country, we can see a staggering void. Economics have all but fallen on the backs of "Middle America"; Education is a failed effort; and our social graces and interests leave a lot to be desired. Many seek to cover their mistakes and shortcomings by writing a check or attending church. These offer false comforts and confirmations of our self-serving behaviors. But if the behaviors were otherwise, would we be faced with the vast amount of challenges like we are?

I recently had breakfast with a new friend who has resolved to leave the lights of her broadcast employer and on-camera career because she is tired of the sensationalism and filler-stories that are being disguised as journalism. Gone are the days of researching, checking facts and telling stories for the purpose of informing. Rather, it's find something that fills the time, occupies minds, and inflames emotions. She is leaving on her own terms to do something, in her opinion and heart, which matters.

I don't know if what my friend will do will make a difference. But, we do what we think is best at the time. I, too, sometimes doubt if my work and words—here and otherwise—do what I intend them to—encourage, inspire, and inform. I then recall the comment of a young lady I met at a conference. We were looking at t-shirts, one of which said "MD to be." I told her of my regret in not pursuing my dream of becoming a doctor. She said that perhaps my words and voice were better served outside of a hospital, and that perhaps where I am is where I am supposed to be, at least for right now.

Success varies in definition and is relative to what one considers important, and meaningful. Yet, for all of the policy and practices set forth, it sometimes boils down to the simplicity of day-to-day decisions, words from a stranger, and actions or reactions that have the biggest impact of all.

# Chapter Six:
## *It's Personal*

*It can be difficult to nearly impossible to not be impacted by the things that you see and hear on a daily basis.*

*At some point, it moves from observation to obsession; an ingestion of all you see, do, and want to make better.*

*Beyond the professional wish and effort, it becomes a personal agenda and preference.*

# TOO PETTY TO PROSPER

I sit and watch, listen and learn, shake my head and wonder why people spend so much time fighting the progress and accomplishments of others. Unfortunately, I have long found myself of the receiving end of such negativity. At first, I blamed it on their youth, but I can now blame it on nothing more than ignorance.

While some think these words are attacks on others, they are simply restraints on themselves. I have been pondering this article for some time as I watch while people exert their time and energy on such pettiness that has no real purpose. It is only an expedient way to self-destruction.

People that prosper—personally, professionally or other-wise--do so because they don't waste valuable time trying to bring others down to the low level at which others perceive themselves. Instead, they invest positive time, energy and effort into uplifting themselves, and others. They genuinely smile when someone else succeeds—even if it's beyond their own—and want well for others as much as they do for themselves; they encourage and celebrate, and feel and show pride for collective achievements, and not just personal gain.

Words and actions, as they should be, are used to support, encourage, nurture and grow the interests and abilities of others, not to tear them down.

From day one, I was taught to never be envious of another. I never had a reason to be, and neither does anyone else. I don't judge people on what they have or have achieved, so it does not become their foremost characteristic to me. I recognize that material things are just that, and are bought and sold every day. Appropriate value should be placed on these things, and not used to determine the person. Things are no reflection of whom or what kind of person others are. People fall into the trap of allowing material things to influence or determine their opinions and perspectives of people, usually mistakenly so.

Comparing oneself to others only yields a false sense of security or insecurity, because there will always be someone who has achieved and acquired more, just as there will be those who have considerably less. The focus should be on you, and what you want to do and acquire without the influence or consideration of others. Sure, we can use the achievements of others as incentives, but not as targets for demise.

Above and beyond is the wasted effort of working against others. Talking about them, harboring negative or ill thoughts, or doing little things that are thought to be happiness or progress inhibitive.

In essence, people who spend time thinking about others and their situations, deplete their own energy surplus that they could—and should—otherwise invest in themselves. It's not possible to help yourself, when your intent is to harm others.

I watch as this person tries oh so hard to be important to others. They want to be respected, admired and looked up to; when the reality is that their pettiness negates all respect and consideration that they may otherwise get. What drives their actions are the accomplishments and possessions of others. Their disdain for those things becomes a negative undercurrent, and determinant of their words and deed. This is insecurity at its best, or rather worse.

My mother used to always say *"Don't dig a whole for*

*someone else, because you may fall in it yourself."* And, therein lies the answer. You cannot pull up to the table from which you desire to feed, if you are using your hands as blockers for others. And, remember that you cannot receive blessings from God if your arms are busy trying to block the blessings of others.

## DETROIT IS NO JOKE

I am a Detroiter. Not a pseudo resident, or one who contingently embraces this city, but one who was born, raised and continues to call Detroit-proper my home. As such, I am fed up and don't find it amusing that so many fair-weather residents or those who selectively embrace this city choose to use it as the butt of their jokes.

While the media has repeatedly placed and kept Detroit negatively in the news now for far too long, the city is no laughing matter. And, I take it personally. I am offended by the fact that some want to call Detroit their home when it is convenient, or when things are going well and are celebratory, but otherwise choose to trash the city, literally and figuratively, and its residents. I also don't appreciate, understand or agree with the fact that living in the metropolitan area makes you a Detroiter. It does not.

People that do not live here might very well enjoy and even contribute to the benefits of this city, and that is fine. They are all more than welcome, and true regional cooperation would be great and ideal. But those who do not live here do not have the same challenges, concerns or interests as those who do. Saying that they are entitled to voice their opinion and make demands as though they live here are without warrant or justification. Detroiters can't even visit parks in surrounding suburban communities, less only make demands about their political process, choices or social and economic circumstances. Aren't we entitled to the same autonomy?

Everybody loves Detroit, but differently. Some love the city for all of its struggles, growth and apparent potential. Others appreciate it for what it was, and still others only want it if it can be what they think it should. But loving something means first respecting it, and then doing both under any circumstances, without compromise. While that does not mean agreeing with everything and everybody, it does mean that destructive behavior and condescending comments are off limits. If it is indeed the heart of Michigan, shouldn't everyone want and work for its well-being? If so, then abusive relationships are unacceptable, even between a city and residents, it's own and others.

It seems that those who most loudly criticize the city, have the least right to do so. Most of them don't even live here, and their concerns are selective and self-serving. That is like the Monday-morning quarterback, and says a lot about one's true interests and concerns, perhaps including only them.

I have never been sensitive to the words and comments of others, instead shrugging them off to ignorance, jealousy or one's willingness to follow others equally so. But, I am tired of the constant bashing of Detroit and its residents. Yes, it is a collective criticism, believe it or not. When they talk about one of us, all are included.

It takes more than simply visiting, wearing Detroit paraphernalia, and appearing emotional about what happens in this city to be a real Detroiter. Should you have any doubts as to whether or not you are, just check your driver's license.

# I WOULD LIKE TO
# BELIEVE

In the year 2008, we have the technology to do things that were once considered beyond reasonable thought, have resources to enable all, and yet we still face the basic challenges of human understanding and tolerance. I would like to believe that things have changed, but wonder if they truly have, or ever will.

In a country occupied by every race and culture, every shade and stance, we still ensure, perpetuate and validate prejudicial comments and actions. They are the basis of comedic performances, and have become a platform for everyday life. Insensitivity to others and their concerns has regrettably permeated every aspect of our being.

Beyond the thoughtless comments made by those in the public, my concern lies with the day-to-day encounters that impact our quality of life, and the lessons they lend to our children. Comments that scream insensitivity and detachment, or maybe just a lack of care and concern.

While talking about the role of diversity for students and the impact that it has, a lady old enough to know better said that of course students should be taught the value of diversity so they can do things like "go out and help the Mexicans." Or, maybe it was the electronic request for help finding people with a "servant" mentality. Intentional? Not necessarily. Freudian? Possibly. Insensitive? Definitely.

As a parent, I teach my children to embrace and accept others as they are, without consideration of anything more than the substance of character. Yet, at the same time, I must teach them that others don't always feel, nor will they necessarily react, this way. I bear the burden of teaching them how to navigate veiled hate and disdain, emerging stronger and undaunted.

I am saddened by the fact that while I encourage and demand excellence from my children, I know that some will seek to taint that excellence because of personal issues beyond our control. These acts and deeds exceed the perimeters once imposed by law, preventing equal access and opportunity. Those small and sometimes overlooked or trivialized words and actions are veiled variations of the same impositions that once kept us all apart.

Today, no laws are necessary. People freely apply and display their prejudices and preferences into their personalities and professional practices without compromise. You never know who or what you are getting, or why.

Centuries after slavery and decades after desegregation, I'd like to believe that we have changed as country, a culture, a people. Yet, we are only days removed from the last prejudicial encounter and sadly, only moments away from the next.

## BLACK REQUIRES BALANCE

Recently, I was having a conversation with someone whose profession is in an area with very few African-Americans. Historically, perceptually and realistically, the numbers of blacks in this particular area are few to non-existent. Yet, this person, while one of only a few, represented a voice and view into an area seldom ventured.

During the conversation, they shared that they spoke the way they did because it resembled those with whom they sought to assimilate. In order to fit in, they explained, they had to adopt certain practices, one of which was speaking and articulation.

I wasn't sure if I was more perplexed, or insulted at their comments, and asked why they somehow felt that speaking correctly was identified with being something other than black. I questioned how they sought to ever make a difference if they bought into the perceptions and prejudices that fueled these beliefs, especially being in a place where they were certainly unquestionably the microcosm of all black folks.

Why, I asked, was it assumed that all non-African-Americans spoke correctly? It is an incorrect assumption. This topic was the tip of the emotional iceberg with this person, as I could see they had some deep-seated issues.

Somewhere along the line, this person, as so many others, lost their identity and connectivity with who they are. They assumed that ascending to a certain level of professional success somehow severed them from, well, themselves.

Black is not synonymous with wrong, negative or unprofessional any more so than being white means the opposite. But, when a person of color travels across social, professional or economic lines, it requires a delicate balance.

Without compromise or apology, many blacks must find ways to maintain their cultural identity and connection while tolerating and engaging in other ones. Some even adopt a primary and secondary personality. One, usually evident in mixed company, is where they are articulate, professional, quiet, socially conscious and culturally reserved. The other enables them to relax a bit, if you will, with the comfort of knowing that their comments, actions, and articulations will not be so harshly judged, if at all.

The real challenge, however, is for those who find themselves in places or around people who see them as representatives of an entire race and culture, to know that they don't have to jump ship to sail in other waters. Pretending to be something other than what you are only fools you; others are not convinced, impressed or moved. It also depletes any possibility for respect from others. After all, how can you respect someone, no matter what their role, who has not enough respect for themselves to own up to who and what they really are?

# Chapter Seven:
## *Family*

*Of all of that life has to offer, nothing is more important than family.*

*Growing up and moving on should only bring you closer to those you love.*

*So give thanks for those friends who are like family, and family who are friends, and bless those who have moved on and are not with you, whether by of death or decision.*

*The times are short, making memories all the more special. At some point, they may be all you have.*

# SIMPLICITY IS HER SECRET

It was a quiet summer day, and Estelle Smith, or Ya-Ya as friends and family affectionately know her, began the day that marked her 90th birthday as usual—quietly, with prayer and appreciation. While she won't admit to it, and barely looks a day over 16, she goes through her days with a peaceful simplicity that is enviable, and could quite possibly be credited for her longevity and youthful spirit.

She continues to call the neat two-story house on the west side of Detroit her home as she has now for more than 50 years. It is here that she and her late husband, Samuel, raised four children. It is here that she has watched a once tight-knit neighborhood deteriorate into a fragmented collection of strangers, dotted with drug houses and chop shops. Yet, it is also here that she continues to raise a garden right in her front yard that would rival any horticultural showcase.

The squirrels and birds amazingly and without provocation come to her, eat from her hand and the food she leaves for them on the porch, as they, too, find solace in her presence. She doesn't shoo away the bees and yellow jackets that her flowers attract; instead, she allows them to gently land on her shoulder, where, they, too rest comfortably.

Her conversation is lively and entertaining, and she boasts, "Life is great." She doesn't complain about her days alone, the nighttime noise, or a society so filled with fear and hate that it seems beyond imagination or repair.

You don't ask, but have to wonder what is her secret to this inner happiness that radiates from her infectious smile, and the blessing of independence that she still owns and proudly displays. Yet, the answer is obvious: she generously credits God for all that she has, and willingly shares with others. And, she keeps her life simple and uncluttered by today's technology, gossip, and the like, that otherwise clutter one's existence.

She approaches everyday, as we all should: like it is an unpainted canvas ready for the hues of today's experiences, accented by its regularity. She leaves yesterday's worries behind, and knows that tomorrow isn't promised, and lives as such.

The simplicity of her living is so evidenced again by her elation with a bouquet of colorful helium balloons that we brought for her birthday. She ties them to her porch and kisses them. She is thankful for the company, and yet another day that she has been allowed to spend on this earth. And, for those who know and love her, so are we.

## TOO BUSY BEING GROWN

Noticing a billboard on the expressway, my daughter recently asked my sister if she had ever tried pomegranate juice. My sister replied no, but that she remembers enjoying the actual fruit as a youngster. She went on to say that she wishes that she had one now, but that they were just too messy.

My thoughts raced to what it was like opening up the red pomegranate fruit, and picking and eating the individual juice-filled pulps inside. Sure, it was messy, but it was also so uniquely good that it was worth the time it took and mess that it made. We made it a game, and enjoyed the treat. Why wouldn't we eat one now? Why is it a bother and imposition to do something that once brought us joy?

It reminded me of something that my late Grandmother use to say, that we were "too busy trying to be grown." We didn't want to be the children that we were, enjoying what that time and excuse offered to us. Too bad that being grown now equates with sacrificing those things that may actually keep us young, even if only in spirit and makes us remember not appreciating them more at the time.

I began thinking of those things that I used to so much enjoy, but no longer do. Playing jacks, the paddle-ball, drawing on the sidewalk with chalk, lying on the grass and looking at the clouds, chewing bubble gum and continuously trying to blow a bubble bigger than the last, and swinging. I never noticed an age requirement or limitation on any of those things, and I have to admit that I miss them. Although, I have been known to stop and take a swing or two.

I sometimes think that if I had known how hard it was being an adult, I would have enjoyed being a child more. But, youth looks different when you're there. It seems awkward and ill prepared; you're unable and unqualified to do anything, or so you think.

You want to hurry to drive, date, handle your own money, do what you think is best without the input of parents of caregivers. Not so fast, young'un. The other side of it includes bills, responsible behavior, decisions, choices, responsibility, and more than you ever imagined.

People often ask if you could go back to a certain year in your youth, would you and which one would it be? Well, knowing that it's not possible logically prevents me from intelligently asking the question. But, I would only go back if I could take with me what I now know. Had I only listened to those who tried to tell me to enjoy the summers of my youth.

So, while adulthood is here to stay for as long as life will allow it, a nice ripe pomegranate, a game of jacks and a good swing will now have to be remedy enough for days long past.

## UNHAPPY MOTHER'S DAY

It is exactly four days until yet another Mother's Day, one of the most celebrated days in the country where everyone stops to pay homage to his or her mother. For the past eight years, I have had little to celebrate other than the memories of my mother whom I lost in 2000.

I watch as preparation begins for various celebrations, and somehow feel left out and even envious. Not due to the lack of celebrations, but rather the absence of my mother. I never knew the pain and depth of a loss, until I experienced one of my own. When I learned of the passing of a friend's relative or loved one, I would send a card and my condolences, totally unaware of the void and emotional toll of death. Not until I arrived there did I understand.

It's a place almost indescribable, filled with emotion, questions and even anger. I regularly relive the four months preceding my mother's death as she lay dying in a hospital bed unable to speak. I search my mind for what were really her last words, instructions, and encouragement to me. It was a horrible time, as her voice was part of my being. We talked everyday, and all of the time no matter where I was in life, literally or figuratively. I am even guilty of still dialing her telephone number, knowing she will never again answer.

Life without a mother is a place that is untouched by time; the very thing that everyone says will heal the pain. It doesn't. I remember the vast feeling of helplessness, not knowing anyone to call upon to reverse the situation. No amount of money, associates, friends or favors mattered. Prayer even took on a new dimension, as I used it to ask God for a reprieve. When my request was denied, I figured there was no sense in praying anymore, especially since we were subject to the will of God, regardless of what we asked.

I have a different perspective and sensitivity to the loss of others; I now understand and share my insight. I have learned that there is no predetermined period of mourning. For me, it is endless. I accept that no day will ever pass without thoughts of her, and that tears will flow whether there appears to be a reason for them or not. Feelings don't come with or fit a template, so I allow myself to feel, cry and to be, period. And, life goes on.

My sister and I regularly recall what my mother would say or do in situations we witness or encounter. We try to guess how she'd react to seeing her grandchildren growing like the weeds she once plucked from her garden. We quote her favorite sayings, and wish that she were here. These offer short-lived moments of comfort where we relish in her memory, and her presence that remains in our hearts.

I know now what it means to experience a loss, and remind others to appreciate family, friends, and mothers, too, while life permits. Death is an unavoidable but difficult part of life, not for the deceased, but certainly for those left behind.

# *A purpose, a difference*: **Fannye Dumas Parham** *(1925-2000)*

When I was asked to write this piece on my mother, celebrating her as a woman of purpose, I was overcome with
several emotions. First, I was honored that my mother's
contributions and commitments were considered worthy of
this recognition; second, I felt disappointed that it was being done posthumously, and that she was not with us to enjoy it; lastly, I became confused, as I was unable to
immediately limit and or define her one
single purpose.

I had most of my lifetime to watch my mother and witness
her commitments and the results thereof. Yet, I have had
the past two years since her death to reflect on the importance of her words and deeds.

I cannot examine her purpose without looking first in the
mirror and at my family, because nothing was more important to her than us. With family being first, her purpose is
evident in all that I am and do. Her commitment to making
sure that we functioned on principal, with ethics and integ-
rity has allowed personal and professional growth on solid
and sincere soil.  That soil now serves as a foundation on
which my children are standing, and will continue to grow.

I see my mother's purpose in my son's easy-going and
carefree nature; I see her purpose in my daughter's focus
and sincerity; when I listen to words of encouragement and
advise that I often share with others, I hear my mother's
purpose; when I stand and speak up for what I believe is
right even when others choose to remain silent, I feel my
mother's purpose. My sister's patience and my brother's
dignity are all evidence of my mother's purpose.

At the same time, I think of causes and other individuals to whom she was also committed.

My mother was not a Nobel Prize winner, nor was she ever really publicly recognized for all that she did. Rather, she went quietly about her way of making a difference in the lives of all she touched. There were her students at Lingemann Elementary School, whom she taught both from and without books. She taught them about life, from the simple things about hygiene to the more complex message that poor is nothing more than a state of mind. She gave them time and attention, and taught them self-love, all of the things that would make a difference in their lives.

She was the woman, who gave to those less fortunate than her, not just materialistically, but of herself. She shared wisdom with those who were less wise; she shared direction with those who were lost, and she shared encouragement with the downtrodden. I always saw my mother as a giver. She was able to give, because she had so much to share; others were able to accept because they felt her sincerity and concern with their well-being.

She taught objectivity without being blind; she taught fairness without being a pushover; she taught humor without being silly; she taught patience without procrastination; and honor without arrogance. She made friends feel like family, and strangers feel like friends. I use to joke as a young adult that my mother was nicer than I would ever want to be. I couldn't figure it out, until now.

Her purpose was to make a difference in the little boy whose mother was an alcoholic, but who today owns his own business because my mother believed in him and taught him to do the same; to read to a blind mean neighbor when no one else would; and, to teach others to, no matter what, make a difference in your world.

She had the uncanny ability to see beyond the immediate appearance of a person or situation, and the unbelievable spirit to never judge another. My mother would be the listening ear to my fellow high school students, who didn't exactly care for me too much, but who knew my mother did not expect such sound judgment from a teenager, and gave them the ear that they needed.

One of her favorite sayings was that no matter what you've done, you did not invent it, nor would you be the last to do it. So, deal with it and move on. Her unwillingness to judge people created a level of comfort with people from all walks of life, from the guys that spent their days in front of the neighborhood party store to those in the NBA to Rap and Rock stars. She treated them all equally, and they loved her for it. Looking down on or up to others was not something she did.

My mother's purpose was to make a difference. Not the monumental difference that everybody notices and publicly admires, but the kind of difference that most people shy away from because they underestimate its importance, or because there is seemingly no recognition or reward for such.

But, as I look around and see the difference she has made—in my family, others, and me--near and far, and I realize that her purpose was to make the kind of difference that actually *made* a difference. She did, and continues to as those who she loved and touched go about our lives armed with her lessons and now sharing and perpetuating her purpose--to make a difference, one person at a time.

# Chapter Eight:
## *People & Places*

*There is something special about everything.*

*The people we encounter, and the places where we find ourselves each have something unique to offer, if we'd only take the time to look.*

*A word, lesson, or lingering thought or glance can always be the catalyst for further discussion, progress, and growth.*

*And a stranger or friend can also lend a word or experience that can last or shape a lifetime.*

# EVERYTHING IN TIME

She remembers the Klu Klux Klan, being denied equal access, and all the things that we can only read about in history books. He skin is tight, her energy high and her memory as sharp as a tack. On October 14, 1902, Carrie Belle Golden was born in Uriah, Alabama. Just two weeks ago, she celebrated her 100th birthday. At a time when our tomorrows are less than promised, and we bury friends and neighbors younger and younger every day, the celebration of becoming a centenarian becomes even greater. She has been a Detroiter since 1942, and seems to have made a friend every day since.

Although she lost her husband, Osman Hendreith, in 1993, she smiles and laughs like a giddy teenager when she recalls the day that they met. It was at a school softball game one June afternoon. He used to work for her father, who was one of the wealthiest blacks in their county. Osmund was "good looking" and he said when they met that he was going to marry her. And he did the following December. Their marriage lasted 68 years until his death, and brought forth five children. She still brags about how good a person and wonderful provider for their family that he was. He always called her "mother" in hopes that their children would do the same. The children never did, opting to call her mama instead.

Her insight is simple, yet deep. She speaks about how the black community stuck together when it had to, and cites the breakdown within our community as the result of our divisive social options. "When we had to work together, we did so very well," she said. "We depended on each other, because we had to, and we could."

She is the last surviving sibling of her 14 brothers and sisters, and recalls having to bury them as an emotional test of strength and faith. Her parents instilled faith in God and commitment to family, two characteristics that she holds true today. Her life's creed is to be kind to everyone and never hurt the feelings of another. The most impressive thing about her mission is that she actually lives it. She recalls a neighbor who cursed, no make that cussed, her out about having cut a shrub or something equally minor. Mrs. Hendreith never retaliated, and only responded by saying that she was going to pray for the lady. Time passed, and upon every encounter, Mrs. Hendreith spoke to the lady. Without fail, she spoke without having the greeting returned. Finally, the lady asked her why she spoke to her in spite of her having cursed her out and never spoke in return. The lady then showed up at Mrs. Hendreith's kitchen door with a heavy heart and an apology.

If only life were this simple. "But it is," says Mrs. Hendreith. If everyone would simply put their faith in God and treat others the way they want to be treated, everything would be fine. So, while people run around scurrying about their day in a frenzied attempt to get as much, do as much and be as much as they can; while they buy books and what they believe to be remedies for what ails them, their life and society, the answer lies simply there for us all to see and live. The proof lies in the years, and the life she affectionately refers to as "beautiful." "I have given my best, and had the best given to me in return," she boasts." So, having everything is possible...in time.

# OPRAH'S NEW SCHOOL: INSULT OR INSPIRATION?

With much hoopla, entertainment mogul Oprah Winfrey recently unveiled the results of her personal investment of $40 million: a 28 building campus, described as luxurious to say the least, to house and educate 150 South African girls. There was the media frenzy stumbling over the official ribbon cutting, and a few of her star-studded friends came out to show their support. But, not soon thereafter, Oprah's halo seemingly began to tarnish.

Not one with very many critics in the past, Oprah now finds herself with many who are criticizing her decision to invest millions into education in another country, when the same system here is deteriorating, at least. She has said in both published and broadcast reports that she was tired of going to inner-city schools, and eventually just stopped. She spoke of how students in the United States asked for electronics, gym shoes and material goods when she offered to help. That was all they wanted. While those in South Africa asked for uniforms, a requirement to attend school there and get and education. They wanted nothing more.

Many have questioned her choice to make this international investment, with criticisms of her apparent racial and gender-specific decision, to why she is condemning American children for being victims and now poster-children for the very thing she promotes on her show and in her magazine—consumerism.

While I am no fan of Oprah, I am fair. The reality is that Oprah has the right to invest her money whenever and wherever she deems appropriate. On one hand, she makes a point, albeit a veiled one, about the lack of respect and value that we have for education in this country. But, on the other hand, she also has a responsibility to a community that lives like she once did, and looks like her, and now looks to her for inspiration and guidance, if nothing more than by example. Many say she owes nothing to anyone. That is untrue. She cites and recites too many clichés about her ancestors, and those who blazed trails before her not to realize that she, too, is or should be creating a trail on which others—like her—can and should follow. African-Americans don't have the luxury of making it without reaching or giving back. There is too much left undone.

Rather than be insulted by the fact that Oprah chooses to lavish out goods such as diamond earrings at a weekend long celebration of...her, cars to audience members, horses to friends, and fame on seeming strangers, perhaps we should be inspired. Inspired to, with or without her, work harder and make education the priority that it should be in urban communities across the country. Maybe her message is, "See what you all **could** have had if you acted right?" A strange and twisted approach, but perhaps one nonetheless.

So, rather than folks getting mad, perhaps they should get even. Get involved. Create a new standard in education, and help our children achieve it. Show Oprah and the world that it can be done, with or without them. After all, success is, indeed, the best revenge.

# SEE LIFE THROUGH THE EYES
# OF A CHILD

I had the pleasure of attending the grand re-opening of the Domino's Pizza on Woodward in Detroit last week. That alone was an enjoyable experience. It represented a commitment and investment by the Kelley family into the city that we all love and want to continue to see flourish. There was food, drink and plenty of people—invited guests and passersby. There was also a clown who was making things with balloons to the delight of many.

The clown and his balloons were magnets for children. They stood there for what seemed like forever in awe of his ability to create magical animals and things from these strips of un-inflated plastic. I watched, especially, as a little girl stood before him and watched endlessly and without distraction this clown and his endeavors. What captured my attention most were her eyes. They were wide and did not blink, for fear of missing a moment of this fascinating man and his creations. I watched her as she watched the clown. Then I watched the clown, and wondered what she saw.

I began to remember what it was like to see colors that danced in front of my eyes rather than blinded me with their brightness. I recalled the fascination with simplicity, when happiness and contentment did not need to be fueled by complexity and excessiveness. I tried, for a moment, to see the clown and balloons the way I thought this little girl did. I tried to pretend that I was seeing these bright colors of his costume and balloons if not for the first time, one of only a few times before. I looked at the clown and pretended that he was not a man in costume, but really a clown—whose sole purpose in life was to make me happy. I watched as he made animals and figures with balloons, pretending that I did not know the outcome of his creation until he presented it with a "Tah-Dah." I waited with patience as though I had nothing else to do, never once looking at my watch.

When I heard a siren blaring down Woodward Avenue, I looked up to watch the truck speeding down the street. I watched the lights and listened to the blaring sound, and didn't give thought to the severity behind them. I thought of the excitement, and not the sadness with which I knew was associated with someone's illness or injury.

I then heard an ice cream truck, and allowed the melody to dance through my mind, engaging memories that had become dormant. Rather than being bothered by a sound heard by an adult as annoying, I enjoyed the bells, whistles and the images of ice cream cones and summer days.

I looked again at the business, but this time as a child. I didn't give thought to the dollars invested or generated, the jobs brought or the tax base that this entity represented. Instead, I thought only of the pizza, and the wondrous way that it all came together. As I watched them prepare one, I thought not of the planning, measurement and preparation, but rather simply the goodness that was the result.

I simply looked around, and tried to see things differently. Simpler, and less complex than we do as an adult. When you look at the eyes of a child, their eyes seems clearer, eager to see what the world has to offer. Look into the eyes of an adult, and you can see the toll of years and the evidence of sterility. Gone are the eagerness, compassion, innocence and fascination with the simple joys of life and living. Present, instead, are disillusionment, callousness and indifference. We become blinded to, rather than by, the wonders that life has to offer.

So, next time you look at life, look closer. Take the time, close your eyes and remember. See life through the eyes of a child.


## SO LONG, JIMMY

I have not figured out if goodbyes are harder when they're unexpected or planned. Either way, they're challenging, at best. For at least 18 or 19 years, I faithfully patronized Clifford Custom Tailors and Cleaners in downtown Detroit. Tucked away in a once forgotten part of the city, James "Jimmy" Kosmides was an excellent provider of service and a friend to many. While I'd like to think that I'm special, being able to claim Jimmy, his skills, smiles and kind words for myself, I couldn't. Anyone and everyone who came in contact with Jimmy shared the same belief and feeling of being special

After more than 32 years on Grand River and thousands of satisfied customers later, Jimmy closed his doors forever one December 24th. It seemed that he had become a victim of the very progress that he long fought for and wished for and even contributed to—the rebirth of downtown. Jimmy was there when times in the city were good, bad, and worse. Then, being downtown was becoming hip again. And, there was no room for those who worked and waited for things to turn around. Ownership is taking precedence over public demand, and the building's landlord wanted Jimmy out. In spite of reassurances over the years that a lease was not necessary and that the business that Jimmy loved and labored for so long was safe, reality screamed otherwise. That was not progress, to me.

Every Christmas, I brought Jimmy a small gift--champagne, cookies, or some small but sincere gift. It was just my way of letting him know how much I appreciated him. He was always just a nice guy. He would never accept tips—doing an excellent job and the satisfaction of his customers was tip enough. An admitted shopaholic, I would go in, literally, with bags of items that I had collected while waiting to find time to get to Jimmy.

We often laughed at the wonderful deals I'd gotten on my shopping excursions, and he'd share similar stories of the deals that his daughter had found. I'd tell him how I found comfort in knowing I had flexibility in what I could buy because he would always make it work—and fit perfectly!

You can really get to know a person in the several minutes it takes to fit your clothes, especially when those minutes span over many years. I can mark the length of time that I had known and loved Jimmy by my life's events—from being single, dating my husband, getting married, having children, my mother's illness, her death, my career changes and growth. Now, life continues without the sprinkles of kind words and smiles from Jimmy. He was happy when things were great, and shared words of encouragement when they were not. He offered only a peek into his life— his wife, son and daughter, his mother and her battle with the illness of aging; his love of his native Greece, and his unfaltering love and commitment to this city and its people.

I thought long of what gift that I would give Jimmy on what would probably be the last Christmas that I would see him. I decided to give him a hug, look him in the eye, thank him and wish him well. And, I did. I shared a copy of this article, and hoped that it would somehow convey all that Jimmy had done and meant to me over the years, and for all of our friendship that I would continue to carry with me as our lives moved on, albeit separate and perhaps never to cross paths again. But, in case they did cross and because I don't like to say goodbye, I'll simply said, "So long, Jimmy. So long." Downtown Detroit will never be the same without you.

## WHEN THE END COMES TOO SOON

Once upon a time, people grew up, had children, and raised them. Then, after a long and satisfying life, those children buried their parents. It was never supposed to be the other way around. But, life has a brutal way of rewriting itself, defying what we want and think should be the norm. It's a pain and anguish I pray to never know. But as a parent, I cannot help but respond to the losses of others, fearfully though only mentally putting myself into their shoes.

As a parent to a teen and a 'tween, I hear their conversations and discussions about who's who and what's what. I listened recently as they talked about a young man at my son's school who was ill. My son told a part of the story as shared by one of his teachers; my daughter talked about all of the messages on Face Book® and her friends who were pulling and praying for this young man's speedy and complete recovery. I could feel the care and concern that they shared with their peers.

I realized that many of these young people had never been faced with the serious illness of someone their own age. They treated it seriously, but approached it with the optimism found only in one's youth. Death wasn't an option. There were games to attend, a prom to plan, a life to live. They expected a full recovery, and that this young man would soon, again, be back and enjoying his senior year of high school.

A few days later, I listened as hope turned to shock and sadness as word spread of the death of 17-year-old Brandon Spight. A senior at University of Detroit Jesuit High School, his end came just days before his 18<sup>th</sup> birthday. I never met Brandon, but seemed to after hearing and reading all the things that so many young people from around the city were saying about him. As a parent and part of the tight-knit U of D family, we all share in this loss.

He was fun, a phenomenal golfer on the U of D golf team, had a great smile, and was a friend to many his peers declared. This sadness hit close, as my own children and their friends felt this loss. There was talk and tears, and I was reminded of just how innocent some of our young still remain. Even though they have heard, they were never touched by the loss of a friend or schoolmate, as so many other young people are these days.

It is said that life is what gets in the way when you've made other plans, and I guess this is no different. There is no such thing as an untimely death, because, at least for those left behind, there is no such thing a timely one.

# Chapter Nine:
## *Shopping Tales*

*Shopping can be quite revealing—about who you and others are, want to be, used to be, or will never become.*

*From those who serve you, or not, and the shopping practices of those you watch, a lot can be learned about a person.*

*As quiet as it is kept, shopping can be the truest telltale sign of them all.*

# POOR IS AS POOR DOES

While the word poor is commonly used to assess one's wealth or lack thereof, I sincerely believe that poor is a state of mind. People may be broke or be limited in their resources, but how one thinks and acts dictates whether or not those circumstances can or will change things to their benefit, or lock them into an ever present situation of economic compromise.

This came to mind the other evening as I stood in line at a store that I have literally been in only twice, each time to get an audio and then video release for my daughter made available exclusively to this particular retail establishment. There was a guy in front of me who was with a woman I assumed to be his wife and a small child. Their order consisted of what appeared to be the makings of an Easter basket—stuffing, small toys and tons of candy. Going solely on their appearance alone, they did not appear to be awash in wealth. The order totaled $130. His credit card was denied. He asked to process some of it, which was approved. It took two other credit or debit card attempts to pay the balance. This was crazy, I thought, as I mentally tried to justify the necessity of the items in his order.

While I understand the desire to provide for one's children, I fail to understand trying to pay for something that you clearly are unable to afford. Perhaps a smaller amount, or something more meaningful would have been appropriate. I began taking a tally of what this purchase could mean—deeper debt, too much candy, unmet dental needs, and the list continued to grow. While not knowing their particular circumstances, this is a scene that is played out all too often—people spending money on things they very well could, or perhaps should, do without.

These are a few of many practices that lead to a deeper placement of financial circumstances that many say they seek to remove themselves from. I remember someone saying that only black people and poor people pay full price for things. Their pride mistakenly gets in the way of seeking a good deal, while those who can afford to pay are usually the hagglers and *keen negotiators*. But, financial hardship knows neither color nor boundary. The couple in line before me was white. But, African-Americans continue to fuel the economy and help financially sustain every other culture but their own.

Times are tough. Money is tight. This is not the time for any normal person to over-extend himself or herself into financial oblivion. Holidays, birthdays, special occasions, or even weekends, for some, should not dictate a reckless abandonment with limited finances. Lavish graduation parties for kindergartners, over-the-top funerals, and outlandish and overpriced outfits are unnecessary.

The mindset of those who have money and those who don't are drastically different. Perhaps that is some of what separates those who have from those who don't. But, the act of moving from one side of the economic divide to the other is as simple as giving thought to the necessities, planning for tomorrow, and buying what is needed and doing without what isn't. Sure, it sounds simple, but presents an obvious challenge to many.

This mindset and the appropriate actions allow those who don't have to continue to sustain the accounts of those who do, taking poor from state of mind to action. Just take a look at who is on which side of the sales counter.

# HOLD THAT THOUGHT

One of my favorite activities, be it holiday or not, is shopping. It's my hobby, my form of relaxation, and my drug of choice. This Christmas, I decided to be very deliberate and selective in my shopping and selections thereof. We decided to go to Chicago to do our shopping. We made a list, and for the most part stuck to it.

In spite of my decision to limit my otherwise reckless and haphazard shopping activities,
I found it to be quite a funny, insulting, sad and surprising experience. I am sometimes too quick with the tongue, so I held my thoughts to some of these asinine things, and will share some of them with you instead:

The season sillies began when a couple of staff members and I went to Somerset—a mall that I reluctantly visit-- to get the Mayor a Christmas gift. We had an idea of what we wanted to get, but were still open to ideas. I bumped into the General Manager of one of the other stores in the mall—a store that I won't mention. We exchanged niceties, and I told her of our purpose. She put her fingers on her chin and said, "Well, let's see. He's not independently wealthy, so..." I stopped listening after that. I wanted to, but refrained from saying "You are wearing your name on your shirt. Neither are you." How snooty, I thought.

On to Tiffany's we went. This year, they asked that customers looking at "regular" merchandise take a number. I decided that "regular" meant less than $5,000, since it was on the lower level of the store. I found this method rather insulting, but it paled in comparison to being told, "There is no waiting on these items" which were those $150 or less. You know, the kind that many of the Somerset undesirables—those who are not welcome-- seek to buy, I thought.

How "selective." Our desired item was not in the book, so we waited.

Another incident brought me into a jewelry store where the first comment made to me was the question whether I was there to "make a payment." On what, I thought. What happened to "may I help you?" or is it assumed that all of "us" are there to "make payments?" Anyway, while in the store, I overheard another transaction. A young lady had made a purchase of approximately $150. During her transaction, she asked for "the slip that tells you how much clarity is in the diamond." Thinking, but again not saying, "There is no clarity in a $150 diamond." That's extra.

I was making a purchase in yet another store. The cash involved $10 bills. The little old lady quickly pulled out her counterfeit marker and began marking the bills. My thoughts yelled, "I wouldn't waste time making counterfeit $10 bills. They would, at least, be $50's."

Let's try lunch at the famed, but overrated, PF Chang's at Somerset (*sorry, Makeba*). My friend and I were seated, and the waitress looked at us sheepishly and asked, "Have you eaten here before." I thought, gee, am I at Somerset or in Tibet? I just looked at her, and my blank stare must have fueled her agenda. "May I suggest something?" Sure, I said. Go right ahead. Knock yourself out. She went on to say that eating here was "different" and then talked about the most popular dishes that they offered. I wanted to, but didn't say, how different can any domestic restaurant be? You read the menu, make your selection, eat, pay and leave. Did I miss something? I looked at her, hoping she could read my mind. I kept my mouth closed, not wanting to waste my time or words on this stupid woman or her conversation.

To wrap it all up, there were the insulting sights of so

many—too many—young African-Americans in droves at Burberry and Louis Vuitton. The actual door to the Burberry store was literally blocked by those that I think that I can safely assume could be doing something more positive with their money. Not until rappers Big Tymers and Bow Wow began sporting the old plaid did the urban dwellers see fit to do the same. And, at the LV store, I shook my head in disbelief as I watched these kids mull over the designer bags and shoes. The scent of marijuana filled the air, and do-rags were plentiful. Sure, they are entitled to shop and buy this stuff. But, it was just a reminder to me of how our priorities are still not in order. On top of how people still treat us, shopping or otherwise, we really have to give more thought and action to that which we choose to do.

I'm not just thinking this one. I am saying so.

## Forty Years of HOPE

This year has a significant meaning for the word hope, an unseen but paralleled vision set forth forty years ago by two groups committed to making a difference. Founded in the wake of the Detroit riots in 1968, Fr. William Cunningham and Elenor Josaitis set out to bridge the racial divide by creating Focus: HOPE.

The organization has since touched and shaped the lives of thousands through training and various forms of subsidized support. What better way to eliminate racial tensions than to prepare the underserved to compete and take control of their own lives. These things offered something less tangible, but far more productive. It brought hope.

I recently joined thousands of other supporters at the 34th annual Walk for Diversity. Any walk or ride down Oakland Blvd where Focus: HOPE is located brings back memories for me of the last walk for Fr. Cunningham in 1996. I remember watching him stand on the balcony of the Church of Madonna, as I marveled in his relentless dedication to this community and his unwavering belief in change. Elenor Josaitis picked up the baton after his death in 1997, and continues that dedication and commitment today.

Forty years ago, there was another hope taking shape. Senator Robert F. Kennedy delivered a radio address on Voice of America where he said, in part, that the country was realizing changes in race relations at a rate where a "negro" could one day be President of the United States. While there is some question as to the actual timing of his delivery and specific content, Kennedy and his family were also beacons of change, believers in justice, and carriers of hope.

Today, we are seeing the results of having hope. Senator Barack Obama is the first African-American to receive the nomination from a major political party for the office of President of the United States. His campaign has run on and encouraged that which fueled the founders of Focus: HOPE and which inspired Senator Kennedy to see beyond this country's immediate circumstances and hues.

How ironic, or coincidental, that these things happened in the same year, one when turbulence, unrest and inequality were the norm. When many thought that things would not, could not, or even for some should not change, Fr. Cunningham and Elenor Josaitis proclaimed that Hope would make a difference, and it did. Sen. Kennedy envisioned a change so drastic, one where this country would truly become the "united" states of America.

Hope, when combined with commitment, and a willingness to work to make a collective difference is a wining formula for all.

# Chapter Ten:
## & Then Some...

*Some of the following are considered non-categorical, but no less interesting than the others.*

*While hard to categorize, they, too have a story to tell, an idea to share, and a lesson to be learned.*

*So there are those, and then there are some more.*

# RESPECT IS TIMELSS

Not too long ago, I had the opportunity to speak to a group of girls at a local Detroit Public Middle School. We had the opportunity to talk about some things that I wanted to—school, family, friends and the importance of education and excellence. I talked about how the expectations of them by some were low, and that it would be up to them to raise and exceed the bar. I shared with them how they already had three social strikes against them—they were black, female and from a large urban community. The perceptions of those characteristics alone could be, if they allowed them, disheartening.

I also spoke of their strength, and that they were equipped to do whatever they wanted to do, regardless of how hard or impossible it may seem. I went on to tell them how they had to always be the best, because there may be times that they may be the only person upon which they can depend.

Then, it was their turn to talk about those things they thought were important. The subject turned to boys, their peers and family situations that seemed challenging at best. If I remember correctly, this is the age where boys and girls begin to recognize each other, but was taken aback by the level and intensity of their interests, involvement and this conversation.

I was concerned with how much of their time these boy-girl relationships seemed to occupy. They spoke of relationships that they witnessed between their mothers, aunts and cousins. I heard stories of how these girls witnessed sexual encounters between adults, and others their age. They talked about it so casually that it was scary. The more frightening thing was that these situations were shaping these young girls views on men, sex, relationships, and themselves.

I recalled this time spent with these young girls the other day when I heard a local professional speak of her own encounter with an abusive relationship, as well as her witnessing one that ended in the death of an associate. She was one of several women being honored at the Black Women's Contracting Association luncheon, of which I was Mistress of Ceremonies.

How, I wondered could a woman end up, or worse yet stay in a relationship that was physically, emotionally or verbally abusive? Without the answer, I know that it happens and continues to plague our community every day. I feared that these students, along with many others, are headed down that road, where men are a goal in life, and are sought and accepted under any circumstances and conditions.

While counseling and legal intervention may work in some cases, the best weapon for women to win against abuse is self-esteem. Our young girls, from day one, must be taught and women reminded that they are worthy of respect, and **not** being respected is never an option.

With contrasting images seeping from videos, television, and even the streets, it's a hard but necessary lesson that must be learned early and often. It helps to build a woman, and may one day save her life.

## THE HIGH PRICE OF FREEDOM

In case you have not noticed, freedom isn't free. As a matter of disappointing fact, it isn't even affordable for most. In a country whose foundation was allegedly built upon freedom and diversity, it has become more and more obvious that freedom is selective, and permitted only when one conforms. Freedom, and the principles therein, are being used more and more by individuals and organizations-public and private—to adhere to what is believed to be right and fair. Or, free.

The City of Warren and neighboring residents in Detroit recently voiced its opposition to a proposed strip club on Eight Mile. While the area is zoned industrial, which allows adult entertainment, those who fought the idea did so on the basis the business being "immoral" and against family values. What that translated into was that it opposed what they thought was moral and right. Somebody, somewhere doesn't believe that this sort of entertainment is bad or wrong, as it is a multi-billion dollar industry.

What if Atheists were to publicly oppose the numerous mega-churches that are springing up all over the city and country? Technically, they could do so on the same basis—their personal beliefs. Paying this level of homage to a being that a select group does not believe in can be viewed as wrong, or bad, at least by the group that holds these opposing views. But, does that make either of the parties wrong? Should the views and rights of one be imposed upon the other?

The teacher at a suburban school recently decided to remove a horoscope column from the school's newspaper because she doesn't believe in astrology or using the stars for "guidance." Well, what about all of the  people that do? What happened to the right to choose, or in this case, read that which is of interest and consistent with one's beliefs?

America has long been presented as the melting pot, with a mixture of cultures and beliefs represented by individuals. But, what good is having these cultures and beliefs, or individuals, if they are not allowed the freedom of expression. Sure, there are laws  and legal perimeters that can and should continue to prevent the rights and opinions and practices of some from hurting others. But, perhaps the country has become too sensitive, realizing during the party that they don't like their invited guests.

We can have or celebrate freedom—of choice, practice, and preference—if one group imposes their beliefs upon another. This can be applied from everything from PETA—the animal rights activist who oppose wearing real fur—to those who push for the Right to Life. Where do the limitations end? Where does freedom really begin?

Passion for one's beliefs is admirable, and even respected within reason. But, with that passion must come the reality that no one person or group holds the key to what is right and just for all. It's not that kind of country. Or is it?

## BLACK? PROUD?

The *Tyra Banks Show* recently featured guests who hated their own race. At first glance, it seemed unbelievable that one would have such self-hatred, and hate those who are like them. But, as I look and listen around, I see evidence of such even without the blatant declaration.

I remember the days of James Brown screaming, *"I'm Black and I'm Proud"* and wonder how much of that rings true today. Listening not only to what is said but what isn't said, I clearly understood why and how some people—especially young ones—can become so easily detached from their cultural umbilical cord.

An African-American man was adamant about his disdain for other black people. He didn't like his color, or those who shared a similar hue. Yet, hidden in his words was his real hatred--for how black people were viewed and treated. I heard him try to hide his search for equality in receptiveness from other races. I also heard his disappointment with how black people were portrayed, or shown. Newscasts, malls, concerts and the like are public stages for fools to show their wares. This, then, becomes the impression that too many assume about people of color, even if they are their own.

A Native American woman spoke of her blame for her heritage for the alcoholism that killed her father, and her view that her people were an imposition to the United States government. She went on to share her stereotypical perceptions of others who shared her race; further fueling an image that Native American's have worked long and hard to shed.

From these two people alone, I see the dangers of buying into the images presented to us as reality. African-Americans are not, nor should be defined, by "Pookie" and "Ray-Ray" on the corner, or Flavor Flav on television. Nor are African-Americans the gangsta image perpetrated by an industry that is exploiting black people at an alarming and expensive rate.

Native Americans are not savages, nor are they an imposition to this country, their country. They are a people with strong respect for their ancestors and heritage, which, too, like their land was ripped from under them. These are clear examples of the dangers of not knowing oneself, first-hand and through the eyes of those who share your skin and experiences. Dangers too, of not knowing the history of one's culture and race. History would totally invalidate the beliefs of both of these people and the many others who share their views, showing them otherwise—that the alcoholism amongst Native Americans was the result of this government's "outreach" and that black was, and remains, beautiful and worthy of pride.

There are plenty of reasons to have pride in being black. Unfortunately, time, circumstances, some entertainers, the media and "Pookie" have simply made them harder to find.

## JUST ONE LAST TIME

Recently, Clare Dougherty, a 13-year old girl from Canton Township, spent several fun filled days skiing with family and friends at a Michigan ski resort. On Christmas Day, as her family prepared to leave the resort, she wanted to go down the slopes one more time before heading home. That last run proved fatal, as she lost control and hit a retaining wall.

On the other side of the world, former Pakistan Prime Minister Benazir Bhutto was rallying in Rawalpindi for the upcoming Parliamentary elections. After speaking to supporters, she was escorted to her vehicle and then driven away. Obviously feeling the fullness of the moment and admiration of her supporters, Bhutto climbed through the vehicle's sunroof enough to wave to her supporters; she wanted to do so just one more time. Her decision proved fatal, as an assassin shot Bhutto before killing himself and twenty innocent bystanders.

As we wrap up one year and head into yet another, many people compile mental lists of the things they think they need to do to make their lives better or happier. The list includes everything from losing weight to earning more money and everything imaginable in-between. But, somewhere in those aspirations, one thing gets lost—living.

Not just being alive, mind you, doing the day-to-day necessities to get you from point A to point B, but, to live, and enjoy every moment despite the challenges, threats, dangers or fears.

Dougherty perhaps enjoyed herself so much that she wanted to end her vacation with the feeling she enjoyed. Maybe she wanted to safely tuck that memory into her pocket for the drive home, knowing she could recall it when things might be less than enjoyable.

Bhutto was Pakistan's opposition leader who was seeking her third terms as prime minister, the first woman of a Muslim nation elected as such. She had just returned to Pakistan in October after eight years in exile. She returned to continue to fight for what she believed, not realizing that it would be her last.

There is a lot to be said for those who face life without fear or apprehension. They embrace life for the opportunity that it is and suck it for all the enjoyment and fulfillment that it is worth. They embrace life, rather than simply live it safely but unfulfilled.

Doing what you enjoy, standing for what you believe, and then daring to do it just one more time, whether it is yet another in a sequence, or the last. Dougherty and Bhutto should inspire us in 2008, because *living* is what life should really be all about.

## RIGHT IS TO LIVE, NOT JUST LIFE

By the time this goes to press, the brain-dead Florida woman who has become the poster child for the right to decide, Teri Schiavo, will either live or die at the hands of an

American government that is obviously confused about its role.

Despite the Presidential and Congressional maneuvering, a federal judge and those thereafter have refused to intervene or reinsert the feeding tube that has kept Schiavo alive for the past fifteen years. This whole scenario raises some questions that I don't hear being asked, or answered.

I first have to wonder, who is paying for all of this? Medically and legally, the bills have to be beyond comprehension. Is it the family, the state, an insurance company, or what? Whoever, I am sure that this isn't all being done for free or out of the goodness of the hearts of the right-to-lifers. Somebody, somewhere has money that could be better spent on a safer and surer medical bet. Think of the unperformed surgeries, transplants and medical attention not administered due to a lack of dollars. Add that to the ever-increasing numbers of uninsured Americans—children and seniors, alike—whose quality of life is severely compromised and shortened due to lack of medical care and attention. Where is the Presidential and Congressional intervention, maneuvering and non-partisan partnering for that?

So, while money, time energy and attention are being focused on Schiavo, there are hundreds if not thousands of Americans who wait for life-saving medical procedures otherwise denied to them for lack of money or public sympathy.

I also wonder why the intense battle between her husband and her parents? With such a fierce struggle between them, their issues go way beyond the traditional in-law rifts. And, while I can certainly understand the emotional struggle with watching a love one decline and not wanting to let go,

I cannot understand nor condone the selfish decision to prolong a life otherwise simply suspended. There is no reason for life if you are not able to live.

These circumstances also scream the reminder to talk and plan with family members about right-to-life issues, end-of-life decisions, and the need for advance directives and a living will. My friend, Probate Attorney Terri Jordan, reminds us, "people don't plan to fail, they fail to plan." And, so it goes.

So the larger of issues surrounding this case is one of quality of life. Having and sustaining someone who is simply alive but not living is cruel and unusual punishment that should not be imposed upon anyone. Schiavo deserves the respect and courtesy of not being exploited for personal or political attention or gain. So, all those including the government who protest and prophesize on the right to life platform should redirect their efforts, and choose to stand on a steadier ground—the right to live.

## MISTAKEN DEMISE REVEALS CARE, CONCERN

It is often said that you don't realize, or appreciate, what you've got until it's gone. Well, last week I encountered a situation that was both eerie and elating. It's hard to talk about a loss, and pair it with any degree of nicety. Yet, that was what happened last week when many people around the city mistook the unfortunate and untimely death of another to be mine.

After a long and rather tiring day, my phone began to ring uncontrollably. Not up for any unnecessary conversation, I ignored the calls, which seemed endless. Then, a number came through that I couldn't ignore. I figured it must be important, and was probably a last minute request to attend a meeting or event. And, while I didn't want to answer this call either, I did.

On the other line was a room full of associates who seemed surprised, yet relieved that I answered my phone. I detected emotion in their voices, as they began to tell me that one of the Council members had mentioned that I had passed away. *What?!?!* Not yet realizing that someone of the last name but no relation for whom I was being mistaken for had actually passed, I responded that they probably wished that I had, but no I didn't.

The conversation took a different turn, as they began to tell me how much they loved me, were relieved that I was OK, and so on. I was flattered. I have shared a mutual admiration and respect with these folks for quite a while. They are wonderful people, and have become like a second family to me over the past three and a half years. We've worked side-by-side as a team for a common goal, learning and, at times, tolerating each other along with the good and bad.

I hung up the phone, nearly in tears. I was touched, to say the very least. The phone rang with similar calls over the next day or so. People calling to make sure that I was OK. My cynical humor wondered why would someone call my cell phone to see if I was dead? Well, guess you have to start somewhere.

We have all wondered, even if only silently, what people will say about us after we are gone, not just from life but also from beyond our present situations. Did we matter, make a difference, or a least a friend? Were we noticed, remembered, and would we be missed?

105

Let this be a reminder to tell those you love that you do, and show your appreciation while the recipient can enjoy it.

While this was an eerie and unfortunate way of finding out, I got to feel the warmth and love of friends and associates whose feelings I'd only assumed. I publicly asked that the concern for me be channeled into prayer for Robin Dumas and her family, and quietly hoped that she once had the chance to realize her impact and appeal before we were no longer able to tell her.


## HANDS OFF MY SUV

A new set of ads hit the airwaves this week targeting Detroit automakers for not being "fuel" conscientious in the manufacturing and marketing of SUV's and what some consider "gas guzzlers." This comes on the heels of the ads attempting to prompt the same conscientiousness by asking, "what would Jesus drive?"

The effort seems to try to stir some sense of guilt and patriotism, neither of which I have.
The former is a wasted emotion, and the latter is another conversation. Regardless, I cannot figure out why everybody is picking on the SUV's.

If I remember correctly, SUV's helped to save Chrysler when no one was buying their product, and SUV's actually helped to "keep America moving." People wanted safer and roomier vehicles, and the manufactures responded. Sales soared and everybody was happy. Now, there's another issue that I cannot clearly define.

Use of excessive gasoline is now being touted as a funding source for terrorism. So, until we move to fuel cell and alternative energy, what are we supposed to do? Drive Pintos? Everybody ride the bus? What? Even those things require gasoline.

I am a proud owner of a 5,000-pound, 7 passenger SUV. I have driven trucks for the last 12 years-- comfortably, proudly and faithfully. I feel safer, and like the ride and space that it offers. My taste and choices have grown with me over the years, moving from practicality to pure luxury. I spend a lot of time in my vehicle, so I want it to be something in which I am comfortable and honestly enjoy. Yes, it uses a lot of gas, but so does my 2-seater whose engine rivals that of the truck. So, what's the real issue here?

Is the issue one of safety, where there are more frequent accidents caused by people who cannot drive, trucks or otherwise? Are the people driving the smaller vehicles feeling left out? Or, must America always have something of opposition on its agenda?

Perhaps it's a ploy to keep us all confused: first, buy a truck, then don't drive it; drink more milk, then milk is unhealthy; exercise, but not too much; play outside, but stay out of the sun; take a pill for what ails you, but take close note of the side effects, which are far greater than your original illness. What's a person to do?

Well, regardless of what "they" say about SUV's, I am keeping my truck and loving every minute of it. I cannot let my transportation choices be determined by someone else's environmental, political or ethical standards.

So, whether we are fueling terrorism, sacrilegious practices or just practicing poor judgment in the eyes of some stands to be determined in the court of personal preference.

And, regardless of what Jesus or anyone else would drive, I prefer my SUV.

## OUTSIDE?!?

To too many of our young people, the word "outside" seems foreign. The mere mention of it brings frowns of confusion and incomprehension. As the weather begins to evolve into spring and then summer, memories of what this time of year used to mean find their way into conversations all around and present a new opportunity of discovery.

A recent Public Television documentary discussed how fear and social dynamics have placed many of our children under house arrest. No longer is going outside to simply play a highlight of their day. Outside has become foreign territory, with unexplored areas that were once fertile and creative grounds for learning. If nothing more, just being— as you once begged to go-- outside was once more than enough.

Gone are the days of riding bikes, playing hopscotch, dodge ball, or a pick up game of any kind with neighboring friends. Walking is an unfamiliar act, replaced by the perception of safeness we find in our cars. And, when was the last time you saw someone climb a tree or roll a tire down the street? Sitting on the porch is frowned upon, and relegated to a condescending socioeconomic category rather than seeing it as an opportunity to talk to your neighbors and sustain a neighborhood bond that protected all that was within.

Even clothes hung to dry outside on the line once represented a game, dodging in between sheets stretched between two lines. It didn't signal that the family couldn't afford a dryer. It meant incredibly fresh smelling sheets when you went to bed after bathing.

Young people today know not the joy of turning an empty washer, dryer or refrigerator box into a car, boat or make-shift slide. Hard rains once brought hopes of clogged sewers, because that meant playtime in the street. Sticks and stones were the basis of rhymes, and could be made into anything else the imagination conjured.

Fights were disagreements that were long resolved before the streetlights came on. There were no guns, or holdover anger that involved relatives or weapons. It was worked out, and then it was over. Libraries, recreation centers, parks, churches and even the homes of neighbors were all places for fun and activities, and adults were refuge from harm. Joy was a walk to the corner store, which offered penny candy and Faygo that we happily shared with others. And, television was something that we *might* have watched at night, if we were not too tired from playing outside all day.

The documentary concluded that much of the fear that restricts us in self-imposed. Sure, we face new challenges but none that can compare with that we choose over being outside: television, video games, cell phones and an otherwise sedentary lifestyle. The results have yielded a fatter and more disconnected community. Yet, the solution is simple: Go outside, and take your kids with you. While things are different, you just might be surprised how much things haven't changed.

# ONCE UPON A TIME, THERE WAS TOMORROW

As we look upon the uncertainty of our days because of imminent war combined with the
prevalence of violence within our world, I think about how this impacts our outlook and anticipation of brighter days to follow.

During a recent conversation with an associate about violence in our society, we talked about how as children; we didn't have the uncertainty that children face today. There was no question about whether or not you would be outside the next day to play again with your friends or see them in school after a weekend or summer break. It was a given. There was a level of comfort and security that we had that gave us the confidence that there was, indeed, another day to follow.

Children, and adults, for that matter, do not enjoy that same luxury today. Everything is questionable. Life is uncertain. Tomorrow is unsure. We are inundated with guns, death, and violence. It has become our world.

I sometimes refrain from watching the news, simply because it can become so overwhelming. Each story reported is a bit crazier than the last. What, I ask will people do next? Where does it end? Will it ever? You take these thoughts to bed, and through your day. They become haunts that are ever present, lurking in the back of your mind as you try so desperately to remain positive and upbeat under seemingly impossible odds.

It becomes hard to encourage oneself and each other when you must incorporate the possibility of what we know and now acknowledge as reality.

As we embark upon what seems like an inevitable war, uncertainty rears its ugly head once more. Again, our days along with our existence are questioned. We hear nuclear warfare, weapons of mass destruction and biological warfare, yet we do not know what it all means other than that they jeopardize all of our tomorrows.

I long for the days when you anxiously awoke to a shining sun, jokes from the weatherman, and the biggest question was what would be the most fun things to do for the day. Responsibilities were as simple as chores, and naps were a given, not luxuries.

Life seemed to move at a slower and more deliberate pace. Maybe uncertainty existed even then, too, but perhaps it was masked in youth and oblivion to current events. It was covered by the arms of family—blood and otherwise—and it kept you safe, warm and secure. Current events then were what prompted questions to your mother and what you discussed in social studies to garner an understanding of our world. They didn't seem like blind battles for power that sought to destroy civilization as we think we know it under the front of a subjective definition of "freedom."

The adage that "tomorrow is not promised" now has a whole new meaning. It is no longer just the incentive to embrace today for all it has to offer; it is now, indeed the reality that today is here, and tomorrows might only be found in a memory.

# LEARNING TO SHARE IN A SELFISH WORLD

It is said that everything that you need to really know in life, you learn in kindergarten: courtesy, respect, sharing. Yet, what some fail to learn is the art of appreciation and modesty, as shown by the hoards of unappreciative and greedy people in the world.

Sharing seems to be a natural trait for most, with those less fortunate, as well as with those whom you simply want to divide your happiness. Yet, the number of people who openly and willingly ask and accept for things—material and otherwise—with the return of any sign of appreciation is staggering, and disappointing. It turns sharers into straight givers; it turns receivers into plain takers. And, it makes it harder to understand the psyche of those who refuse to participate in the give-and-take.

It makes it more and more difficult to openly give and share, especially when that which is given falls upon deaf ear and a hardened heart. And, it begins to unfairly rule out those who sincerely could use a giving hand.

I always say that you cannot go through life with a catcher's mitt. Giving is indeed a two way street, as you cannot draw from a well emptied by those before who refuse to re-contribute. And, the most insulting thing is to help, or give to another who forgets, somehow, to say thank you.

While giving is from the heart, and is not or should not be done for the purpose of any accolades or public due, it is not unfair to give or expect a simple thank you. It validates the gestures of both giving and receiving. It engages the giver and receiver, and emotionally completes the transaction.

Whatever happened to the simple act of saying thank you? Where has the reciprocation of kind acts gone? It is said that those famous three words, "I love you," are those hardest spoken in the English language. Well, I beg to differ. There are two words harder than those three—"thank you."

It's time to revisit our lessons of childhood, and add appreciation to the list. Giving is from the heart, and so should be receiving. For, if giving is an art, then graciously receiving is a masterpiece.

Printed in the United States
213169BV00001B/12/P

9 781432 711306